Ambrosianum Mysterium:
The Church of Milan and its liturgical tradition

Vol. 1

GN00472351

by
Prof. Cesare Alzati

Lecturer in Church History and the History of Liturgy,
University of Pisa

translated from the Italian by
George Guiver, C.R.

Lecturer: Liturgy, College of Resurrection, Mirfield
and the University of Leeds

GROVE BOOKS LIMITED
RIDLEY HALL RD CAMBRIDGE CB3 9HU

Contents

1. The Milanese Church and the Tradition of St. Ambrose 3
2. Liturgy—Rite—*Mysterium* 10
3. The Origins of the *Ambrosianum Mysterium* 16
   1. Pre-Ambrosian structures
   2. Ambrose as presiding over the liturgy of the Milanese church
     a. The daily office
     b. The eucharistic celebration
     c. The ordering of lessons and catechesis
     d. Christian initiation
     e. Gradations of ministry; ordination
     f. Rites of matrimony and consecrated virginity
     g. Penitence
     h. Rituals for illness and mourning
     i. Cult of saints
     j. Dedication of churches
4. The *Ambrosianum Mysterium* between Late Antiquity
   and the Early Middle Ages 37
   Historical background
     a. Continuity and evolution in initiation rites
     b. Dedication of churches and ordination of bishops
     c. The morning office and its Irish connections
     d. The eucharist
     e. The lections in the Ambrosian tradition

NB: Each chapter is concluded with a 'Bibliographical Note'

The **Cover Illustration** comes from the apse mosaic in St. Ambrose's Basilica, Milan (6th-8th century), and shows St. Ambrose celebrating the eucharist at a round altar

A TWO-VOLUME PRODUCTION
This Study provides the first half of a larger treatment by the author. Volume II will be published in this series in 2000

Copyright © Cesare Alzati (translation copyright George Guiver)

First Impression December 1999
ISSN 0951-2667
ISBN 1 85174 421 5

1

The Milanese Church and the Tradition of St Ambrose

The Ambrosian rite is the form of worship used in the most populous Roman Catholic diocese in the world, as well as in some other neighbouring areas. Use of the Roman rite is not allowed in parish churches (many Religious Communities use the Roman rite, except when they have a parish, in which case they have to use the Ambrosian rite; there are also pockets such as Monza which have used the Roman rite for many centuries).

Visitors to a Milanese parish will find the eucharist largely familiar, but will be totally lost in the divine office. They will not find any mass celebrated on Fridays in Lent; and they would not be able to celebrate Ash Wednesday—they may have left Turin in sackcloth and ashes only to find the Milanese still enjoying Carnival until the following Sunday. We are not dealing with a local *Use*, nor even just with different liturgical forms: rather are we dealing with an all-embracing ecclesial culture, steeped in and conscious of its great and venerable tradition, a tradition which is far from dead.

Because of this, it would be misleading to go straight into an examination of liturgical forms and ceremonies. These first two chapters therefore introduce the reader to the towering figure of Ambrose in the context of Milan, and to the all-embracing culture which stems from him.

——————————————

Unusually, church calendars of both east and west commemorate St Ambrose not on the date of his death, but on 7 December, the day in 374 when he was ordained bishop and began a ministry that from its start was seen in the Christian community as absolutely unique. This was partly due to the unusual circumstances of his election as successor to the Cappadocian Auxentius who for almost eighteen years had been a key figure in the anti-Nicene party in the west.

'Auxentius having died . . . there were riots at the announcement of his successor. It was the duty of Ambrose to calm the disorders, so he went to the church. As he was addressing the crowd, it was said that suddenly a child's voice was heard: "Ambrose—Bishop!" Hearing this, the people started to shout with one voice: "Ambrose—Bishop!" Arians and Catholics had till then each sought, for their own advantage, to have him as their own bishop, but suddenly they found themselves united in a miraculous and incredible concord.'

Whatever credence we want to give to Paulinus' account (only later was he a colleague of Ambrose[1]), some words of Basil to the new bishop show how

---

1   PAULINUS, *Vita Ambrosii*, VI. 1; dependent in its turn on Rufinus, *Historia Ecclesiastica*, XI

3

contemporaries saw these events which had brought the provincial consul, still a catechumen, from a ruler's seat to the bishop's throne:

'Remember, therefore, O man of God, that it was not humans who gave or taught you Christ's gospel, but the Lord himself has taken you from among the judges of the earth to place you on the seat of the Apostles'[1]

As a magistrate Ambrose had already established official relations with the cities of the neighbouring provinces of Liguria and Aemilia, and so more or less the whole of Italia Annonaria (Northen Italy) became a vast ecclesiastical province looking to the bishop of Milan. The exceptions were Flaminia and Picenum Annonarium, which were suburbicarian sees, and above all Aquileia, a port of singular prestige in the italic context, testified to by the presence of the Imperial palace (and of it we shall hear more shortly).

But this was not all. The bishop of 'the first Italian See', who according to Augustine was indeed Bishop of Italy[2], was not slow to intervene in disputes involving the greatest see of all, Rome, where in concert with bishops of the Council of Aquileia Ambrose asked the Emperor to take action against Ursinus[3], rival of Pope Damasus; but there were similar interventions in Constantinople[4], Alexandria[5], and Antioch.[6] It was in the west, however, that Ambrose's prestige became greatest, as an arbiter in questions of discipline and doctrine, from Spain[7] and Gaul[8] to Illyricum.[9] Ambrose's decisions carried permanent canonical authority in Spain, and the Illyrian Bishops (led by the bishop of Thessalonica) together with their opponent, the heretic Bonosus[10], even appealed to him against a decision of a suburbicarian Roman synod.[11]

It needs to be noted that this 'care for all the churches'[12] was not due to Ambrose's personality, however unusual that was. It was inconceivable without a clear and widespread conviction that he was competent to intervene, together with his synod, in questions which troubled the Christian communion at that time.

---

1   BASIL, *Epistula* CXCVII. 1.
2   AUGUSTINE, *Contra secundam Iuliani responsionem imperfectum opus*, I.59.
3   AMBROSE, *Epistula* e. c. V [Maur.: XI]
4   AMBROSE, *Epistula* e. c. IX [Maur.: XIII]
5   AMBROSE, *Epistula* e. c. VI [Maur.: XII]
6   AMBROSE, *Epistula* e. c. VI [Maur.: XII]; *Epistula* e. c. IX [Maur.: XIII]; *Epistula* LXX [Maur.: LVI]
7   over the Priscillianist movement: PRISCILLIAN, *Liber Ad Damasum* (*Tractatus secundus*), 50-51; SULPICIUS SEVERUS, *Chronica*, II.47.5.
8   over the Felician schism: AMBROSE, *Epistula* e. c. XI [Maur.: LI]; Ibid., *De obitu Valentiniani*, 25
9   over anti-nicene resistance: PAULINUS, *Vita Ambrosii*, XI-XII. 1; THEODORET, *Historia Ecclesiastica*, IV, 7. 6-9. 9
10 over the heresy of Bonosus: AMBROSE, *Epistula* LXX [Maur.: LVI]
11 AMBROSE, *Epistula* LXX [Maur.: LVI]; on relations with the see of Thessalonica cf. also *Epistula* LI (Maur.: XV); *Epistula* LII (Maur.: XVI).
12 PAULINUS, *Vita Ambrosii*, XXXVIII.2.

In fact, even before Ambrose Milan had occasionally been the venue of important ecclesiastical events and episcopal assemblies, and even Ambrose's successors, Simplicianus and Venerius, continued to exercise, alongside the Roman Pope, the role of highest point of referral, be it for the churches of Gaul, Africa or Spain.

A council of Carthage in 404 enables us to see the reasons for this peculiar status. Sending its own resolutions as usual to the church across the sea, its bishops said,

'for the accreditation of our legates let letters be sent to the bishop of the Roman church and the other bishops of the places where the emperor is to be found'[1].

This authority had much in common with the status of Constantinople set out by the Council of Chalcedon:

'the city honoured by the presence of the Emperor's authority . . . becomes, even in ecclesiastical matters, equal to Rome, and second only to her.' (Canon 28).

After the departure of Honorius and his court from Milan in 402 the Bishop ceased to exercise this role he had for decades fulfilled. The area of his authority also shrank as Aquileia and Ravenna rose in importance from the early fifth century. The prestige of the see of Milan, however, did not suffer, the voice of its bishop and suffragans (who at the end of the fifth century were going to Milan to be ordained[2]) continuing to make itself felt in the great ecclesiastical controversies of late antiquity, from Nestorianism to Monophysitism, from Symmachus to Acacianus, from the Three Chapters dispute to the Monothelite crisis. A few decades after Ambrose's death, amid heated doctrinal discussions in the Christian Oikumene, the Milanese metropolitan and his synod saw themselves as guardians of a secure tradition of orthodoxy, identified, for them, with the magisterium of Ambrose.

In fact in 431, shortly after the Council of Ephesus, John of Antioch and other oriental bishops with a leaning to diiphysitism, wrote to Rufus of Thessalonica pointing out that, in respect of the current dispute, 'Martinus [=Martinianus] the Bishop of Milan, most holy and dear to God' had sent them a letter, and he had similarly 'sent to the most pious emperor a book by the blessed Ambrose on the Incarnation of the Lord'.[3] This reference to *De incarnationis dominicae sacramento*, and more generally to the magisterium of Ambrose as a paradigm of sure orthodoxy, was not only found in Milan. In 451 the Province's bishops under their metropolitan, the Greek Eusebius, solemnly received Abbondius of Como, and Senator, a Milanese presbyter and member of the western mission to the east preparing for the Council of Chalcedon. They informed Leo of Rome that they had received a copy of the *Tome of Flavian* from Ceretius of Grenoble

1 Corpus Christianorum Latinorum, CXLIX, p.213
2 ENNODIUS, *Vita Epifanii.*
3 In *Acta Conciliorum Oecumenicorum*, I: I, 3, pp 41-4

and had recognized its splendid orthodoxy—'in all senses it shows how far the blessed Ambrose, moved by the Holy Spirit, introduced in his books the Lord's incarnation.'[1] We can see in these fifth-century episodes the seed of that Ambrosian identity which would lead Gregory I to speak of the Metropolitan of Milan as 'Vicar of Ambrose', and the Milanese clergy as 'servants of Ambrose'.[2]

In the Carolingian period, probably at the time of Archbishop Angilbert II (824-859), an anonymous cleric who liked to style himself 'the last of the servants of Ambrose born in his house', described the bond between the church of Milan and its ancient bishop:

'In Christ Jesus he begot us by means of the gospel; in effect, anything of virtue and grace in this Milanese Church is without any doubt derived from his teaching, by God's intervention.'[3]

This way of seeing things comes out in the term 'Ambrosiana ecclesia' found in texts like this[4], and in later documents such as a letter of the Roman Pope John VIII.[5] This identification with Ambrose was characteristic of the *scientia Ambrosiana* cultivated in the schools attached to the episcopal church of Sancta Maria, finding its most coherent expression in the work of the so-called 'Landulfus', probably of the early twelfth century. For him Ambrose is 'our apostle'[6], 'the first and greatest to rule from the metropolitan throne'[7], giving the Milanese Church its norms of faith, institutional order, canonical discipline, and liturgical forms and books (cf esp. Book I).

This rooting in the tradition of Ambrose was never lost in the medieval centuries, and found a new vitality in the post-Tridentine period with Charles Borromeo: the ecclesiology of the Council's texts paid close attention to the particular responsibilities of bishops and their collegial responsibilities in the local churches. From his consecration on 7 December 1563, and before he had received the office of Archbishop, Borromeo, seeing himself as already having this office through his consecration, adopted for himself the use of the Ambrosian rite. He was deeply inspired by the patristic episcopal model, and saw himself as a successor of Ambrose and steward of his heritage. His contemporaries saw him as a 'new Ambrose', and revered him as such after his death.

In fact Gregory spoke of Ambrose's successors as 'vicars' in a similar way to the papal relation to Peter, described by Caspar as 'mystische Personalunion'.[8] A recent expression of this came in a sermon by Cardinal Giovanni Colombo at the Ambrosian festivities in 1979 on the occasion of his retirement. Following

1 PL, LIV, c. 946..
2 Gregorii I *Registrum*, XI, 6 (a. 600).
3 *De vita et meritis Ambrosii*, 95-96, ed. P. Courcelle, *Recherches sur saint Ambroise. Vies anciennes, culture, iconographie* (Etudes Augustiniennes, Paris 1973), p 121.
4 *Ibidem*, 67, p 99.
5 MGH, Ep Karolini Aevi, V, N° 269, p 237.
6 L(andulfus), *Historia Mediolanensis*, III, 24 (23): MGH, SS, VIII, p 91, 18
7 L(andulfus), *Historia Mediolanensis*, I, 1: p 37, 30-31.
8 E. Caspar, *Geschichte des Papsttums*, I, Tübingen 1930, p 264.

Paulinus, he told how some newly baptized candidates, entering into the basilica after the death of Ambrose, had seen him still alive sitting on the *cathedra* in the apse. Cardinal Colombo made the observation that

'The eyes of the children who had just come from the font of regeneration were able to sense the mystery which has given vitality and continuing youth to this Milanese church through the centuries: her bishops pass away worn out by years of struggle and hard work, but under the varied and ever-changing aspects of their service Ambrose, a strong and gentle father, a wise and spiritual master and an incomparable pastor, remains always with us.'[1]

It is within such a tradition as this that the unique liturgical heritage of the Milanese church is planted and rooted. And even if today the Ambrosian tradition is limited to the liturgical sphere, its liturgical texts and ceremonial forms enable us to hear the echo of an ecclesial reality in which doctrine and canon, spirituality and institution are organically interwoven, giving substance to a network of significant relationships with other churches of the Christian communion.

---

1   'Rivista Diocesana Milanese'. LXXI (1980). p 87

Bibliographical note

On Milan in the eastern empire: M. Sordi, *Come Milano divenne capitale*, in *L'Impero romano-cristiano*, Rome 1991, pp 33-45; Ibid, *I rapporti di Ambrogio con gli imperatori del suo tempo*, in *Nec timeo mori. Atti del Congresso internazionale di studi ambrosiani nel XVI centenario della morte di sant'Ambrogio*. Milan, 4-11 April 1997, Milan 1998 (Studia Patristica Mediolanensia, XXI), 107-118. **On the position of the city's bishop in this imperial context:** C. Alzati, *"Ubi fuerit imperator". Chiesa della residenza imperiale e comunione cristiana tra IV e V secolo in Occidente*, in *L'Anglicanesimo. Dalla Chiesa d'Inghilterra alla Comunione Anglicana*, Genova 1992, pp 21-39 (also in *Ambrosiana Ecclesia. Studi su la Chiesa milanese e l'ecumene cristiana fra tarda antichità e medioevo*, Milan 1993 [Archivio Ambrosiano, LXV], pp 3-21). On the make-up of the Milanese metropolitical province: C. Alzati, *Genesi e coscienza di una metropoli ecclesiastica: il caso milanese*, in *Historia de la Iglesia y de las Instituciones Eclesiásticas*, M. J. Peláez (ed), Barcelona 1989 (Trabajos en homenaje a Ferran Valls i Taberner, X), pp 4085-4105; also in *Ambrosiana Ecclesia* (op.cit.), pp 23-43. **On the Milanese church amid the great debates of late antiquity:** C. Pasini, *Le discussioni teologiche a Milano nei secoli dal IV al VII*, in *Diocesi di Milano*, I, A. Caprioli, A. Rimoldi, L. Vaccaro, (eds) Brescia-Gazzada 1990 (Storia religiosa della Lombardia, IX), pp 43-82. On Ambrose's successor the Cappadocian Auxentius, and on the 'arianism' of which he and all the other anti-Nicenes were accused by their enemies and by subsequent historiography: C. Alzati, *Un cappadoce in Occidente durante le dispute trinitarie del IV secolo. Aussenzio di Milano*, in *Politica cultura e religione nell'Impero romano (secoli IV-VI) tra Oriente e Occidente*. Atti del secondo Convegno dell'Associazione di Studi Tardoantichi. Milan, 11-13 October 1990, Naples 1993, pp 59-76; fuller notes in *Ambrosiana Ecclesia* (op.cit.), pp 45-95.

Regarding **Ambrose**, a detailed bibliography has been published by the 'Dipartimento di Scienze Religiose' of the Catholic University of Milan: *Cento anni di bibliografia ambrosiana (1874-1974)*, Milan 1981 (Studia Patristica Mediolanensia, XI); **for a critical assessment of available historiography:** G. Visonà, *Lo status quaestionis della ricerca ambrosiana*, in *Nec timeo mori. Atti del Congresso internazionale di studi ambrosiani nel XVI centenario della morte di sant'Ambrogio*. Milan, 4-11 April 1997, Milan 1998 (Studia Patristica Mediolanensia, XXI), pp 31-71.

Any understanding of the events surrounding St Ambrose inevitably depends on the written sources; that condition, which affects all historical research, puts a question mark over suppositions based on unverifiable claims about intentions, and resulting historical reconstructions which may make sense, but are no less arbitrary for that. These **methodological questions** are raised in a recent monograph by N.B.McLynn, *Ambrose of Milan*, Berkeley-Los Angeles 1994. Regarding the episcopal election in particular, seeing it as orchestrated by Ambrose (H. F. von Campenhausen, *Ambrosius von Mailand als Kirchenpolitiker*, Berlin-Leipzig 1929, pp 27-28) or as manoeuvred by the Prefect Probus and indirectly the emperor Valentian (cf. C. Corbellini, *Sesto Petronio Probo e l'elezione episcopale di Ambrogio*, "Rendiconti dell'Istituto Lombardo. Classe di Lettere, Scienze Morali e Storiche", CIX [1975], pp 181-189) clearly relies on forcing the textual data. On the election itself and the substantial plausibilty of Paulinus' account: Y. M. Duval, *Ambroise, de son élection à sa consécration*, in *Ambrosius Episcopus. Atti del Congresso internazionale di studi ambrosiani nel XVI centenario della elevazione di sant'Ambrogio alla cattedra episcopale*. Milan, 2-7 Dicembre 1974, II, G. Lazzati (ed) Milan 1976 (Studia Patristica Mediolanensia, VII), pp 243-283; R. Gryson, *Les élections épiscopales en Occident au IVᵉ siècle*, in Revue d'Histoire Ecclésiastique, LXXV (1980), p 322.

On Ambrose's reputation in the east: G. Galbiati, *Della fortuna letteraria e di una gloria orientale di sant'Ambrogio*, in *Ambrosiana. Scritti di storia, archeologia ed arte pubblicati nel XVI centenario della nascita di sant'Ambrogio*, CCCXL-MCMXL, Milan 1942, pp 45-95; on the Greek sources: C. Pasini, *Le fonti greche su sant'Ambrogio*, Milan/Rome 1990 (Opera Omnia di Sant'Ambrogio. Sussidi, XXIV, 1); on the Russian tradition: E. M. Verescagin, *Il culto di sant'Ambrogio di Milano nella letteratura slavo-ecclesiastica e nel popolo russo*, in *Un ponte tra Occidente e Oriente. La visita di Bartolomeo I a Milano—Atti del Convegno "Ambrogio tra Occidente e Oriente" (15-18 Maggio 1977)*, Milan 1998, pp 171-179; the Romanian tradition: N. Vornicescu, *La vita e l'opera di sant'Ambrogio vescovo di Milano nel culto della Chiesa rumena, nella spiritualità e nella cultura rumene (sec. XIV-XX)*, in *Un ponte tra Occidente e Oriente* (op.cit.), pp 125-169.

On the memory of Ambrose in late antique and early medieval Latin sources: A. Rimoldi, *La figura di Ambrogio nella tradizione occidentale dei secoli IV-X*, "La Scuola Cattolica", CIX (1981), pp 375-416; G. Banterle, *Le fonti latine su sant'Ambrogio*, Milan/Rome 1991 (Opera Omnia di Sant'Ambrogio. Sussidi, XXIV, 2). On the *De vita et meritis Ambrosii*: P. Tomea, *Ambrogio e i suoi fratelli. Note di agiografia* *milanese altomedioevale*, "Filologia mediolatina", V (1998), pp 149-201. The letter of *Gregorii Magni Registrum*, XI, 6 (a. 600), ed. D. Norberg, I, Turnhout 1982 (CCL, CXL, A), p 868, was used probably in the opening years of the 12th century by L(andulfus) [= Landulfus, *Historia Mediolanensis*, edd. L. C. Bethmann, W. Wattenbach, Hannover 1848 (MGH, SS, VIII)], II, 9, p 49 (on the author, title and date of this work, see below). On other attitudes earlier than this cf. Humbertus a Silvacandida, *Adversus Simoniacos*, III, 9, ed. F. Thaner, Hannover 1891 (MGH, L. d. l., I), p 210. **On the history of the definition *vicarius Ambrosii*:** Arnulfus, *Liber gestorum recentium*, I, [2], ed. I Scaravelli, Bologna 1996 (Fonti per la storia dell'Italia medievele ad uso delle scuole, I), p 60. 23; *Commemoratio superbiae Ravennatis archiepiscopi*, ed. L. C. Bethmann, Hannover 1848 (MGH, SS, VIII), p 12. 57. On the latter text cf. E. Cattaneo, *La tradizione e il rito ambrosiani nell'ambiente lombardo medioevale*, Appendix: *La questione del primato d'onore fra Milano e Ravenna, in Ambrosius Episcopus. Atti del Congresso internazionale di studi ambrosiani nel XVI centenario della elevazione di sant'Ambrogio alla cattedra episcopale*. Milan, 2-7 December 1974, II, ed. G. Lazzati, Milan 1976 (Studia Patristica Mediolanensia, VII), II, pp 41-47 (also in ibid., *La Chiesa di Ambrogio. Studi di storia e di liturgia*, Milan 1984 [Pubblicazioni dell'Università Cattolica. Scienze Storiche, XXXIV], pp 153-159); P. Tomea, *Tradizione apostolica e coscienza cittadina a Milano nel medioevo. La leggenda di san Barnaba*, Milan 1993 (Bibliotheca erudita, II), pp 34-43.

On the many problems relating to so-called **Landulfus (Senior)**: J. W. Busch, "*Landulfi senioris Historia Mediolanensis*"—*Überlieferung, Datierung und Intention*, "Deutsches Archiv", XLV (1989), pp 1-30; but on the date see C. Alzati, in *Ambrosiana Ecclesia*, pp 212-214, note 20; cf. ibid., *Chiesa ambrosiana, mondo cristiano greco e spedizione in Oriente*, in *Atti del II Convegno internazionale di cultura nel IX Centenario della I Crociata (1099-1999)*, Bari, 11-13 January 1999 (shortly to be published). The *Scientia Ambrosiana* (L[andulfus], II, 35: MGH, SS, VIII, p 70. 15), as already remarked, had a privileged place of transmission in the schools of the Bishop's church of St Mary Major; on these educational institutions: A. Viscardi, *La cultura milanese nei secoli VII-XII*, in *Storia di Milano*, III, Fondazione Treccani degli Alfieri, Milan 1954, pp 721 ff.; A. Majo, *Dalle scuole episcopali al Seminario del Duomo*, Milan 1979 (Archivio Ambrosiano, XXXVI), pp 36-42; T. Schmidt, *Alexander II. (1061-1073) und die römische Reformgruppe seiner Zeit*, Stuttgart 1977 (Päpste und Papsttum, XI), pp 8-10.

On Charles Borromeo as **"alter Ambrosius"**, besides the biographies which directly witness to his life (A. Valier, *Vita Caroli Borromei*, Verona 1586, pp 57, 91-99; G. P. Possevino, *Discorsi della vita et attioni di Carlo Borromeo*, Rome 1591, pp 121, 124, 140; Giussano, *Vita di S. Carlo Borromeo*, Rome 1610, pp 52-53), see the numerous accounts collected by G.A. Sassi, *S. Caroli ... Homiliae*, V, Mediolani 1747, pp 304 ff. **On the Borromean understanding of the Ambrosian tradition:** C. Alzati, *Carlo Borromeo e la tradizione liturgica della Chiesa milanese*, in *Carlo Borromeo e l'opera della "grande riforma". Cultura, religione e arti del governo nella Milano del pieno Cinquecento*, eds. F. Buzzi/D. Zardin, Milan 1997, pp 37a-46b. On the necessary distinction between the Tridentine and Post-Tridentine phases: P. Prodi, *Note sulla genesi del diritto nella Chiesa postridentina*, in *Legge e Vangelo*, Brescia 1972, pp 208-217.

2
Liturgy—Rite—Mysterium

At the 1975 St-Serge conference on the liturgy of the local church and that of the church universal, A.M.Triacca made the following observation: 'we will speak not of the Ambrosian rite, but of the Ambrosian liturgy. The former indicates an ensemble of local church customs and norms of worship, law and government centring on the Metropolitan Church of Milan . . . In this sense the Ambrosian liturgy is a manifestation of the Ambrosian rite.'[1]
We need to be clear about this terminology and the way it is used. The greatest problem concerns the exact semantic import of the terms 'rite' and 'liturgy' and their consequent usage.

Our current use of the word 'liturgy' to mean forms of worship, almost to the exclusion of any other term, has no roots in the Latin tradition of the church. Its foreign nature is evident when it first appears among western scholars in the sixteenth century: their use of it in a eucharistic sense shows the direct influence of patristic and liturgical texts of the Greek-speaking world, then becoming more familiar through a new and passionate apologetic engagement.[2] The increasing popularity of the term since the nineteenth century is inseparable from that new awareness of the theology of worship and a related sense of the Church which were disseminated by the so-called 'Liturgical Movement'. One of the Movement's great promoters, Salvatore Marsili, came in more recent times to see liturgy as 'a word characterizing a whole spiritual attitude typical of the work and new approach initiated by Vatican II'.[3] We clearly have here a strongly ideological approach, comparable with semantic uncertainties present in other authors, and confirming the problematic nature of a term which has no roots in the western Latin tradition of worship, and now being used in a different way from that of its historic Greek-speaking context.

'Rite', on the contrary, can be traced as a Latin term back to the most archaic roots, its meaning clearly expressed by the pagan writer Festus: 'Rite is the approved way of administering sacrifices.'[4] For the patristic period Willibald Plöchl has spoken of 'a term denoting sacred ceremonial.'[5] Even this religious understanding of the word shows a legal overtone specially valued by canon

1   A.M.TRIACCA, Liturgie ambrosienne: amalgame hétérogène ou "specificum" influent?, in Liturgie de l'Eglise particulière et liturgie dell'Eglise Universelle. Conférences Saint-Serge. Paris, 30 juin-3 juillet 1975, Rome 1976, pp 289-290
2   cf. G. CASSANDER, Liturgica de ritu et ordinatione dominicae caenae, quam celebrationem Graeci Liturgiam, Latini Missam appellarunt, Coloniae Agrippinae 1558; J. GRANDCOLAS, Les liturgies anciennes ou la manière dont on a dit la sainte Messe ..., 3 vols., Parisiis 1697-1704; L. A. MURATORI, Liturgia Romana Vetus, 3 vols., Venetiis 1748; and A. M. CERIANI, Notitia Liturgiae Ambrosianae, Milan 1895.
3   S.MARSILI, La Liturgia, momento storico della salvezza, in Anamnesis, I: La Liturgia, Casale Monferrato 1974, p 45.
4   'Ritus est mos conprobatus in administrandis sacrificiis' (Sextus Pompeius Festus, De verborum significatu quae supersunt cum Pauli Epitome, ed. W. M. Lindsay, Leipzig 1913, p 364.
5   'ein sakraler Zeremonialbegriff' (Geschichte des Kirchenrechts, II: Das Kirchenrecht der abendländischen Christenheit. 1055-1517, Vienna 1955, p 59.

lawyers at the time of the crusades, as the western presence in the Levant brought about new contacts between 'Latins' and 'Greeks'. Talk then was of the 'rites and customs of the Greeks', and the Fourth Lateran Council of 1215 directly addressed, in article 9, the question 'of different rites within the same faith'. Here the term 'rite' was beginning to transcend the purely cultural sphere to include the whole heritage of customs, forms of life and canonical discipline found in the eastern churches. This particular meaning appears in the Roman church, especially in post-tridentine ecclesiology, principally to define the connection between the 'Greek' communities in the west (especially in Italy) and their local Latin dioceses; later, and more generally, it was used to refer to the relationships which at that time were resulting from unions established between the Roman Church and individual eastern churches (ecclesiologically demoted to the rank of 'rite'): '*Roman* church and *Greek* rite', the apposite title of a well-known book by Vittorio Peri.[1]

The statement by Triacca which opened this chapter clearly uses 'rite' in this way. Although this may open up new and fruitful ways of looking at the Ambrosian inheritance ecclesiologically, it risks putting the unique Ambrosian tradition in a framework foreign to it. It seems best therefore to look first of all to the sources for investigatory tools—the specifically Milanese sources developed in the context of the '*scientia Ambrosiana*'. Yet again 'Landulfus' is an invaluable and especially insightful guide—in his apologia for the Ambrosian church tradition (building on a wide spectrum of patristic and synodal sources) his aim is to present to future generations the foundations, rationale and splendour of the Ambrosian inheritance, which he saw as by then irremediably compromised. In fact, in the situation of conflict between empire and papacy which characterized life in the west in the second half of the eleventh century, Archbishop Anselm III had in 1088 abandoned the traditional claim to the autonomy and prerogatives of the Ambrosian church and, leaving the communion of Clement III and that part of the episcopate loyal to the empire, he attached himself to the reforming papacy of Urban II. From then on the Ambrosian institutional forms of life and canonical discipline, and especially the ancient local canonical tradition of clergy marriage, were drastically revised, if not completely abolished. And so there began a process which would bring this identity down to the mere level of one variation of the worship found in the Latin west.

Looking back from that decisive moment of change, to what the Milanese church had been, and considering the riches of her tradition, L(andulfus) used two terms which were pregnant with meaning: '*ordo*' ('the blessed Ambrose, whose *ordo* we preserve')[2] and '*mysterium*' ('Pope Gregory brought all the Latin-language churches back to uniformity with the Roman church, but stopped at the venerable Ambrosian mystery').[3] On these two terms, our Ambrosian apologist wrote in the dedicatory epistle to his own work, reflecting on what had taken place in his time: 'The false Cathars, having overturned this *ordo*, have dismantled

1   V. PERI, *Chiesa Romana e Rito Greco*, Brescia 1975
2   'the blessed Ambrose, to whose *ordo* we keep' L(ANDULFUS), *Historia Mediolanensis* III.22 [21])
3   L(ANDULFUS), *Historia Mediolanensis* II.4

it so far that no further hope remains that *mysterium* and *ordo* can be restored.'

Although in effect the organic unity between *ordo* and *mysterium* was beginning to unravel irreversibly, the forms and texts of the *mysterium* itself, the liturgical heritage of the Ambrosian tradition, managed in both forms and texts to survive fruitless attempts on it from the *Patarini* (a prof-Roman reforming party within the Milanese church—the 'false Cathars'). In addition, the awareness of the connection between institutional and disciplinary order and the *mysterium* was not all lost at once. About the year 1130 Beroldus the *cicendelarius* (an officer responsible for providing the extraordinary amount of lighting in the cathedral, and therefore of considerable importance) eloquently witnesses to this. Commissioned by the archbishop to put in writing how the rites of the Ambrosian church were celebrated[1], he found it indispensabe to preface this with a presentation of the church's institutional organization, set out—as in 'Landulfus'— in terms of its ten orders: the priest-cardinals under the archpriest, the seven deacon-cardinals under the archdeacon, who was second only to the archpriest, subdeacons, *primicerius* of the 'decuman' priests ' [L(andulfus)[2] calls him *co-episcopus*] ('decuman' = urban priests with cure of souls, with ring and staff as insignia; '*primicerius*' = head), the notaries ('called acolytes right up to the present day'[3]), sixteen readers plus their *primicerius* , four schoolmasters (*magistri scholarum*), sixteen guards (*custodes*) under the authority of the '*cimiliarch*', the eight senior ones being divided into four *ostiarii* and four *cicendelarii*, twenty ancients (ten men, ten women) who in the name of the people presented the offering of bread and wine at the eucharist, and finally the '*laicalis ferula*' (wand of the representative of the laity) of the '*vicecomes*' (literally, 'viscount').[4]

The liturgical books show how this organization was bound up inseparably with the order of the rite. And because of the connection between ministerial *ordines* and *ordo mysterii* (orders of ministers and order of the mystery), the nomenclature codified by the Roman rite often fails to fit the Ambrosian books. The full celebration of all ceremonies of the official Ambrosian rite took place in the two cathedral churches (St Mary Major and St Thecla, variously known as old/new, minor/major, 'winter'/'summer' churches) and on particular occasions in other churches of the city. All of this came under the responsibility of the archbishop and cardinal-clergy.[5] In such celebrations, where older uses and customs were preserved, the Ambrosian church showed all its ministerial orders in full operation. But alongside this solemn form there were other celebrations peculiar to the pastoral ministry exercised by the 'decuman' presbyters who lived together in colleges in the main churches of the city; then there were more modest celebrations in chapels of various sorts.

---

1   what L(andulfus) called the *ordo Ambrosiani mysterii*; L(ANDULFUS). *Historia Mediolanensis* II.6.
2   L(ANDULFUS). *Historia Mediolanensis* I.3
3   L(ANDULFUS). *Historia Mediolanensis* I.7
4   BEROLDUS. ed. MAGISTRETTI. pp 35-36
5   They were designated with the following terms: *cardinales* / *de ordine* / *ordinarii.*

While from the Carolingian period the *'Liber Typicum'* of the decumans' celebrations—following on from the more ancient *libelli*—was the Missal (but without music), the cardinals' celebrations used a variety of written sources which gave the form of celebrations and the particular ministries within them. So, for example, there existed, besides the sacramentary, particular *rotuli* (literally, scrolls) for the archbishop's and cardinals' celebrations, kept by the *rotularius*. They contained the prayers for vespers, vigils of saints, and for the morning office of Sundays in Eastertide, and for the *Letaniae* (on ordinary feasts and Sundays the *collectarium* was used[1]). Among books for the readings, it is to be noted that there was not simply a gospel-book, but one specific to the deacon-cardinals, containing gospel readings, Pauline passages, *passions* and *depositions* which through the year were read by deacons[2]

The OT lessons for Lenten ferias were in two books proper to the Readers (Genesis and Proverbs). For the first three ferias of Holy Week (*Hebdomada Authentica*) they are condensed for the deacons into two further books (Job and Tobit). The Missal itself, while being the book of the decuman clergy's presbyteral liturgy, preserved as its paradigm the celebration of the archbishop and cardinals—the archbishop is frequently assumed as celebrant, and the meagre rubrics, especially at Easter, explicitly mention the two cathedrals.

A book particularly dear to Ambrosian ecclesial consciousness was the *Manual*, based likewise on the cardinals' liturgy: it is a book which, it would seem, was born in the cathedral school: a minute guide to the daily celebrations, showing the sequence of events together with the chant in full. In the appendix are pastoral formularies for baptism of the sick, penance, funerals, and even trial by ordeal, showing it was used by the decuman and rural clergy.

The musical provision in this book (attested also in a palimpsest from not long after the seventh century) makes it similar to the *antiphonal*, while the details of the daily celebrations make it the predecessor of the *ordo* of Beroldus the *cicendelarius*, which appeared around 1130.[3] The complementarity of Beroldus and the Manual is shown in the work of the priest Giovanni Boffa, who in 1269 wove the former into the text of the Manual, so giving birth to 'Beroldus Novus'.[4]

The particular reference to the archiepiscopal form and the rites of the episcopal churches was not without importance for Ambrosian identity: in effect, every celebration, in whatever place, appeared in the books as a celebration of the Church gathered around the vicar of Ambrose and the ordained servants of Ambrose. In this way the Ambrosian tradition continued to hand on through the centuries the vital connection between *ordo* and *mysterium* basic to its ecclesial identity: a connection still set out in the rubrics—modelled on the cathedral's worship—of the *editio typica* of the Missal of 1902, which was only replaced by new books after Vatican II.

1   BEROLDUS. pp 45. 15. 17. 19. 22; 55. 30; 57. 25
2   see Biblioteca Ambrosiana. Milan. MS *28 inf.* of the ninth century.
3   *Ordo et caeremoniae ecclesiae Ambrosianae Mediolanensis.* that is. the *ordo Ambrosiani mysterii* for the use of the cardinals and archbishop.
4   (Milan. Metropolitan Chapter Library. MS *II.D.2.28*).

Bibliographical note

For an overview of sources on the terms liturgy, rite, *ordo* and *mysterium* in Ambrosian usage, see C. Alzati, *Chiesa ambrosiana e tradizione liturgica a Milano tra XI e XII secolo*, in *Atti dell'11° Congresso Internazionale di Studi sull'Alto Medioevo: Milano e il suo territorio in età comunale (XI-XII secolo). Milano, 26-30 ottobre 1987*, I, Spoleto 1989, pp 396-403, 420-421 (also in *Ambrosiana Ecclesia* [cit.], pp 256-262, 277-278); on the Landulfian use of *mysterium* to mean—as in approximately contemporary Hispanic sources (e.g. Pelagius of Oviedo)—the liturgical heritage of a church as a whole: C. Alzati, *Appunti di lessico medioevale ambrosiano: mysterium nella Historia di Landolfo seniore*, in *Ambrosiana Ecclesia* (cit.), pp 249-253.

On the disciplinary aspects of the Ambrosian *ordo* in the middle ages: *Tradizione e disciplina ecclesiastica nel dibattito tra Ambrosiani e Patarini a Milano nell'età di Gregorio VII*, in *La Riforma Gregoriana e l'Europa. Atti del Congresso Internazionale promosso in occasione del IX centenario della morte di Gregorio VII (1085-1985). Salerno, 20-25 maggio 1985*, II, Rome 1991 (Studi Gregoriani, XIV), pp 175-194; *A proposito di clero coniugato e uso del matrimonio nella Milano alto medioevale*, in *Società, istituzioni, spiritualità. Studi in onore di Cinzio Violante*, I, Spoleto 1994, pp 79-92; *I motivi ideali della polemica antipatarina. Matrimonio, ministero e comunione ecclesiale secondo la tradizione ambrosiana nella Historia di Landolfo seniore*, in *Nobiltà e Chiese nel Medioevo, e altri saggi. Scritti in onore di Gerd G. Tellenbach*, ed. C. Violante, Rome 1993, pp 199-222; also in *Ambrosiana Ecclesia* (cit.), pp 187-206; 207-220; 221-247.

On the organization of the Milanese city clergy in the two *ordines* of *cardinales* and *decumani*, it is sufficient to refer to: E. Cattaneo, *Istituzioni ecclesiastiche milanesi*, in *Storia di Milano*, IV, Fondazione Treccani degli Alfieri, Milan 1954, pp 651-703 (where, in addition, a suggested connection between oriental missionaries operating in tricapitoline Lombardy in the seventh century and the origins of the decuman clergy is shown to be implausible. This hypothesis comes from the research of G. P. Bognetti, partly collected in *L'Età longobarda*, 4 voll., Milan 1966-1968; cf. ibid., *Milano longobarda*, in *Storia di Milano*, II, Fondazione Treccani degli Alfieri, Milan 1954, pp 182-190). On pastoral structures, G. Andenna, *Le istituzioni ecclesiastiche di base sui territori lombardi tra tarda Antichità e basso Medioevo*, in *Storia della Lombardia Medioevale*, Turin 1999, pp 121-164; ibid, *Chiesi, previ e parrocchie (sec. XI-XV)*, in *storie illustrata di Milano II* ed. DELLA PERUTA (Milan, 1992) pp 601-620.

The Ambrosian liturgical books are set out among the collections of Latin liturgical codexes in: C. Vogel, *Introduction aux sources de l'histoire du culte chrétien au moyen âge*, Spoleto 1966 (Biblioteca degli Studi Medievali, I); English translation: *Medieval Liturgy: An Introduction to the Sources*, transl. and ed. W. G. Storey and N. K. Rasmussen, Washington 1986; K. Gamber: *Codices Liturgici Latini Antiquiores*, I, Freiburg, Switzerland 1968² (Spicilegii Friburgensis Subsidia, I); *Codices Liturgici Latini Antiquiores / Supplementum*, eds. B. Baroffio, F. Dell'Oro, A. Hänggi, J. Janini, A. M. Triacca, Freiburg, Switzerland 1988 (Spicilegii Friburgensis Subsidia, I/A). On the Missals, a review can be found in A. Paredi, *Messali ambrosiani antichi*, in *Quaderni di Ambrosius*, suppl. to "Ambrosius", XXXV (1959), pp 1-50, and R. Amiet, *La tradition manuscrite du Missel ambrosien*, "Scriptorium", XIV (1960), pp 16-60; also by the same Amiet on the Manuals: *La tradition manuscrite du Manuel ambrosien*, "Scriptorium", XLIX (1995), pp 134-142.

Among transcriptions of the MSS:

Sacramentary 'of Ariberto' (Milano, Biblioteca del Capitolo Metropolitano, ms. II.D.3.2, early eleventh century, but according to E. B. GARRISON mid-twelfth century—*Early Italian Paintings* Vol. II (London, 1984) p 323): ed. A. PAREDI, *Il sacramentario di Ariberto. Edizione del ms. D 3-2 della Biblioteca del Capitolo metropolitano di Milano*, in *Miscellanea Adriano Bernareggi*, ed. L. CORTESI, Bergamo 1958 (Monumenta Bergomensia, I), pp 329-488;

Missal of Biasca (Milan, Biblioteca Ambrosiana, MS. A 24 bis inf., Late ninth/early tenth cent.): ed. O. Heiming, Münster Westfalen 1969 (Corpus Ambrosiano-liturgicum, II; Liturgiewissenschaftliche Quellen und Forschungen, LI);

Missal of Bergamo (Bergamo, Palazzo Episcopale, Archivio della Curia, ninth cent.): ed. A. Paredi, Bergamo 1962 (Monumenta Bergomensia, VI);

Missal of San Simpliciano (Milan, Biblioteca del Capitolo Metropolitano, MS. II.D.3.3, Late ninth/early tenth cent.): ed. J. Frei, Münster Westfalen 1974 (Corpus Ambrosiano-liturgicum, III; Liturgiewissenschaftliche Quellen und Forschungen, LVI);

Evangelistary and Capitolary of Busto (Busto Arsizio, Biblioteca Capitolare di S. Giovanni Battista, MS. M I 14, Late ninth cent., but with pre-Carolingian arrangement of readings): ed. A. Paredi, *L'Evangeliario di Busto Arsizio*, in *Miscellanea liturgica in onore di Sua Eminenza il Cardinale*

Giacomo Lercaro, II, Rome/Paris/Tournai/New York 1967, pp 207-249;
Lectionary (formerly in Milan, Biblioteca del Maestro delle Sacre Cerimonie del Duomo, early twelfth cent.; the codex, presumed lost, has been tracked down by P. Carmassi, *Ein wiedergefundenes mittelalterliches Lektionar der ambrosianischen Kirche*, "Archiv für Liturgiewissenschaft", XXXV-XXXVI (1993-1994), pp 358-365: Milan, Biblioteca Nazionale Braidense, Fondo Castiglioni, ms. *16*): ed. P. Cagin, in *Codex Sacramentorum Bergomensis*, Solesmes 1900 (Auctarium Solesmense, I), pp 193-207; **Manual of Valtravaglia** (Milan, Biblioteca del Capitolo Metropolitano, MS. *II.D.2.30*, s. XII): ed. M. Magistretti, Mediolani 1905;
BEROLDUS, Ordo et caeremoniae ecclesiae Ambrosianae Mediolanensis (Milan, Biblioteca Ambrosiana, MS. *I 152 inf.*, a. 1140 c.; on the redaction of the codex: M. Ferrari, *Valutazione paleografica del codice ambrosiano di Beroldo*, in *Il Duomo cuore e simbolo di Milano. IV Centenario della Dedicazione. 1577-1977*, Milan 1977 [Archivio Ambrosiano, XXXII], pp 302-307; on the composition of the *Ordo* a few years before, around 1130: G. Forzatti Golia, *Le raccolte di Beroldo, Ibidem*, pp 308-402).

A full and systematic identification of the books used in worship in the Milanese area starting with the oldest witnesses in late antiquity and with particular reference to the categories used in the Ambrosian tradition, has now been completed by Patrizia Carmassi in her doctoral thesis *Liturgische Bücher und kirchliche Institutionen Mailands im Mittelalter. Studien zur Ausbildung des ambrosianischen Lektionars*, which will also appear in the Maria Laach series "Liturgiewissenschaftliche Quellen und Forschungen" with the title, *Libri liturgici e istituzioni ecclesiastiche a Milano in età medioevale. Uno studio sulla formazione del Lezionario ambrosiano*.

Historical Overviews of the *mysterium Ambrosianum*: E.G.Atchley, *The Ambrosian Liturgy*, London 1909; W.C.Bishop, *The Mozarabic and Ambrosian Rites*, Alcuin Club, London 1924; P. Lejay, *Ambrosien (Rit)*, in *Dictionnaire d' Archeologie Chrétienne et de Liturgie*, eds. F. Cabrol, H. Leclercq, I, 1, Paris 1924, cc.1373-1442; E. Cattaneo, *Storia e particolarità del Rito Ambrosiano*, in *Storia di Milano*, III, Fondazione Treccani degli Alfieri, Milan 1954, pp 763-837; A. A.King, *Liturgies of the Primatial sees*, London 1957; P. Borella, *Il Rito Ambrosiano*, Brescia 1964; *ibid.*, *Excursus* on the Ambrosian rite in M. Righetti, *Manuale de Storia Liturgica*, 4 vols Milan 1964³, 1969³, 1966³, 1952²; A. M. Triacca, *Ambrosiana (Liturgia)*, in *Nuovo Dizionario di Liturgia*, eds. D. Sartore, A. M. Triacca, Edizioni Paoline, Rome 1983, pp 16-52; at a more accessible level: *La tunica variegata. Conversazioni sul rito ambrosiano*, ed. M. Mauri, Milan 1995; A. Paredi, *Storia del Rito Ambrosiano*; especially on Daily Prayer: E. Cattaneo, *Il Breviario Ambrosiano*, Milan 1943; G.Guiver, *Company of voices*, London 1988; on the eucharistic liturgy: E. T. Moneta Caglio, *Intendere la Messa*, Milan 1939; E. Cattaneo, *La Messa nelle terre di sant'Ambrogio*, Milan 1964. On Ambrosian chant: E. Cattaneo, *Il canto ambrosiano*, in *Storia di Milano*, IV, Fondazione Treccani degli Alfieri, Milan 1955, pp 580-720; M. Huglo, L. Agustoni, E. Cardine, E. T. Moneta Caglio, *Fonti e paleografia del canto ambrosiano*, Milan 1956 (Archivio Ambrosiano, VII); B.G.Baroffio, *Ambrosianische Lliturgie*, in *Geschichte der katholischen Kirchenmusik*, I.Kassel 1972, pp 191-204; E. T. Moneta Caglio, *Manoscritti di canto ambrosiano rinvenuti nell'ultimo ventennio*, "Ambrosius", LII (1976), pp 27-36. Recently the following very useful source of information has appeared: *Dizionario di Liturgia Ambrosiana*, ed. M. Navoni, Milan 1996.

3
The Origins of the Ambrosianum Mysterium

1. Pre-Ambrosian structures

The legal and institutional structures set up by Constantine were as decisive for the Ambrosian tradition of worship as they were for other places. The week, centred on the *dies solis* as the day of rest[1], the construction of grand buildings for worship in the main cities of the empire, and above all the founding and dedication of the Palestinian sanctuaries, beginning with the great complex of the *Anastasis* at Jerusalem, laid the basis for evolving an organic system of celebrations and rites which would eventually embrace the whole church year.

Already with the Tetrarchs at the end of the second century Milan had become residence of the western Augustus, who gave the city a new circle of walls enclosing a vast area, which beyond the old Augustan walls to the north-east contained only scattered buildings. In the Constantinian era the Christian community built here its first intra-mural basilica.

We are unable to date the beginnings of the Christian presence in Milan: in October 313 its bishop Mirocles was at the Roman Council on the Donatist question[2], and the next year at the Council of Arles with his deacon Severus[3]; the bishops' list for Milan gives five names before his, suggesting a fully-developed hierarchy by the third century. In any case, not many years after the construction of the old basilica (*basilica vetus*) with its baptistery, a large new five-aisled basilica (*basilica nova*) was built nearby on the same axis. It had already been completed in 355 when Constantius II convoked the council at which, in front of a turbulent crowd, Valens of Mursa snatched the Nicene profession of faith from under the pen of the local bishop Dionysius, who was immediately deposed and sent into exile.[4] Later on, Ambrose added a new baptistery based on the design of imperial mausoleums, taking its form from the octagonal basin which by now had become traditional. In this way there grew up the architectural spaces in which the *Ambrosianum mysterium* developed and for centuries would be lived out.

It is impossible to know if and how far this architectural development was influenced by Jerusalem. There were two worship-spaces on one axis, and two baptisteries connected not only with the annual initiation rites, but also with stational moments in the daily offices. It is clear too that many aspects of the Jerusalem pattern of worship were taken up in Milan and adapted in various ways, but we have insufficient evidence on the beginnings and original forms of Milanese worship to be able to say more. Subsequent documents contradict those scholars who support the thesis of Roman origins (sometimes linked to an assertion that the liturgies of all the western churches derive from Rome), while there is

1   *Codex Iustinianus*, III.12.3; *Codex Theodosianus*, II.8.1.
2   OPTATUS Milevitanus, *Adversus Parmenianum* I.23
3   Corpus Christianorum Latinorum CXLVIII pp 14ff.
4   HILARY, *Fragmenta Historica*, App.II.3; AMBROSE, *Epistula e.c.XIV* [Maur. LXIII], 68.

16

some evidence to support Duchesne's hypothesis of kinship with the different forms of liturgy found in the churches of Gaul and Spain. The immediate predecessor of Ambrose, the Cappadocian Auxentius, formerly a presbyter in Alexandria, was in fact represented by the ill-willed Athanasius as ignorant of Latin when, in 356, having been installed in Milan, he began his long episcopate.[1]

In any case, by the time of Ambrose established ritual forms already existed, for he describes the reading of Jonah on the fifth feria of Holy Week as 'according to custom' (*de more*).[2] The pericope from Jn 5.1ff (the paralytic at the pool), present in Ambrose's catecheses to the neophytes preserved in *De mysteriis*[3], reappears in the more problematic *De sacramentis*[4] with the comment, '*lectum est heri* ', suggesting an already-fixed order of lections[5]. Similar considerations count for I Cor 1.21-22.[6] While there was an order of readings which by Ambrose's time had become 'customary' in the Milanese church, it obviously remains an open question when this was established. The same kind of arguments apply to the practice of not fasting on Saturdays[7] (obviously with the exception of Holy Saturday, marked by a great and universal fast at the taking away of the Bridegroom).

The church, therefore, which was entrusted to Ambrose at the end of 374 was a community already possessing its worship-spaces, with at least some aspects of ritual discipline in place, and some texts which at the time of Ambrose seem already to be tied definitively to specific days in the year. The *Ambrosianum mysterium* was therefore not born with Ambrose—its roots go back into church life preceding his arrival.

2. Ambrose presiding over the liturgy of the Milanese church

'In seeing to the things of God he had an extraordinary tenaciousness, to such a degree that at the initiation of baptismal candidates he used to carry out single-handed what could only be done with difficulty by five bishops after his death'.[8]

This comment of the eye-witness Paulinus illustrates the conscientiousness and commitment with which Ambrose fulfilled his role as liturgical presider and mystagogue of the Milanese church. Christoph Jacob has justly underlined how even the exegesis of the Milanese bishop is deeply marked by this mysterical perspective. In fact references to worship appear so repeatedly in his works that a rich tradition of scholarship has grown up which attempts to sift from them the forms and characteristics of the liturgy over which he presided. Here we will limit ourselves to an overall sketch of the available data.

1   ATHANASIUS, *Historia Arianorum*, LXXV.1; *Epistula ad episcopos Aegypti et Lybiae* VII.
2   AMBROSE, *Epistula* LXXVI [Maur.XX], pp 25-6.
3   AMBROSE, *De mysteriis*, IV.22-24.
4   *De sacramentis*, II.2, 3.
5   Cf. *Ibid*, II.2, 9: "*lectum est nudius tertius*" with reference to I Cor 12.4-6.
6   AMBROSE, *De mysteriis*, VII.42; cf. *De sacramentis*, VI.2, 6.
7   AMBROSE, *De Elia* X.34; Augustine, *Epistula* XXXVI [*ad Casulanum presb*.].32; *Epistula* LIV [*ad Ianuarium*].3.
8   PAULINUS, *Vita Ambrosii* XXXVIII.3.

a. The daily office

The hymns Ambrose wrote for his people show an ordering of daily ecclesial prayer through a number of moments in the day: cockcrow (*Aeterne rerum conditor*); dawn (*Splendor paternae gloriae*); the third hour (*Iam surgit hora tertia*); the hour of incense (*Deus creator omnium*). The pillars of this daily cycle were undoubtedly the evening psalms and those at the rising of the sun: 'the psalm is the song of the morning and of the evening.'[1] Ambrose expressly exhorts the faithful to take part:

'Will not anybody who has a minimum of sensitivity not blush at closing the day without the celebration of the psalms, when even the smallest birds accompany the birth of day and night with devout solemnity and sweetest song'[2];

'Hurry in the morning and bring to church the first fruits of your devout prayer ... how much joy is aroused by beginning your activities with hymns and canticles, and with the beatitudes which you read in the gospel!'[3]

In the above words of St Ambrose it is worth drawing attention to the liturgical use, alongside the morning psalmody, of the Beatitudes, an element which subsequently disappeared from the Milanese office.

During Lent there was an afternoon psalmody (perhaps including Ps.CXVIII (CXIX)), which was followed by the celebration of the eucharist; distinct from this was the evening office or *sacrificium vespertinum*:

The fast has been proclaimed. Be careful not to break it; and if hunger presses you to take a daily lunch or intemperance tries to take you away from fasting, preserve yourself notwithstanding for the heavenly banquet. Let not forbidden food draw you aside, lest you be deprived of the heavenly sacrament. Hang on for a while: the day's end is not far off. So much the more in that most days are of this kind, whereby immediately after midday we have to go to church, to sing psalms, to celebrate the eucharistic offering[4]. At that moment in effect you need to be present and ready to obtain a sure defence, to feed on the body of the Lord Jesus, in whom is the remission of sins, the supplication of divine reconciliation and of eternal protection ... the "evening sacrifice" too admonishes you never to offend Christ. When you climb into bed you cannot forget that Lord to whom at the close of day you have addressed your prayer and who has satisfied your hunger with the food of his body'[5].

On certain particular occasions at the time of Ambrose, Vigils were kept, prolonging through the night the prayer begun with the evening office ('while evening was already arriving, we moved to the Basilica of Fausta: there a vigil was kept for the whole night'. So says the *Epistula LXXVII* [Maur. *XXII*] in

---

1 AMBROSE, *In ps.* XII.I; cf. *In ps.* I, preface.
2 AMBROSE, *Hexameron* V.12.36.
3 AMBROSE, *Expositio de psalmo CXVIII*, XIX.32. For the use of the term *hymnus'* in this text see ibid., Prologue, 3: *Titulus psalmi alleluja est: hoc est laus Dei. In his enim hymnis ...*
4 Cf. AMBROSE, *De Ioseph*, X.52: 'It is midday when the true Joseph enters in his house to dine; in effect the day is at its greatest splendour at the time we celebrate the mysteries'.
5 AMBROSE, *Expositio de psalmo CXVIII*, VIII.48.

reference to the translation of the relics of the martyrs Gervasius and Protasius[1]; in *De virginitate* the vigil for the feast of the apostles Peter and Paul is mentioned[2]). The Paschal Vigil, described in Ambrose's mystagogical catechesis in connection with the rites of initiation, is mentioned also by Paulinus in reference to the death of the bishop.[2] Of a quite unique character, obviously, were the vigils in the days before Easter 386, brought about by the struggle for the basilicas with the empress Justina, of which Augustine was a witness; to such dramatic nocturnal psalmody over control of the places of worship is also connected— according to the sources—the introduction of hymns and 'antiphonal singing' of psalms, probably meaning alternating choirs 'according to the normal custom in the eastern regions', and probably with insertion between the verses of short congregational texts sung to their own melody[4].

b. The Eucharistic Celebration

In a letter describing the struggle with the court, Ambrose writes about the events of the Sunday before Easter:

'The next day [the Sunday], after the readings and their commentary, the catechumens having been dismissed, *in baptisterii basilica* (in the basilica by the baptistery) I gave an exposition of the Creed to some *competentes* (baptism candidates). At that point I was told that some of the people had heard that military banners had been sent from the palace to the Portian basilica and that this had flags flying from it (announcing its confiscation), and they had gone down there. For my part, I continued to exercise my ministry. I began to do the *missa* (*missam facere*). While I celebrated the offering, I learned that a certain Castulus had been taken away . . . I then began to weep bitterly and in the offering itself to call on God'.[5]

If, as would seem from the context, *missa* here designates the celebration as such, then we have a use of it analogous to that found in Egeria.[6] From the narrative it is in any case evident that the eucharist celebrated by the bishop was the only one in the city, and that the whole community had been summoned to attend it.

The reference here is to a Sunday celebration; to Ambrose is attributed also the introduction of a daily celebration.[7] This was a development found at this time in other great churches, beginning with Rome and Constantinople. *De sacramentis* explicitly gives an explanation, challenging the different practice more common in the Greek east.[8] The abandonment of a weekly rhythm—which had perhaps involved in Milan as in Jerusalem both Saturday and Sunday—brought

---

1 AMBROSE, *Epistula* LXXVII [Maur. XXII] 2.
2 AMBROSE, *De Virginitate* XIX.124ff.
3 PAULINUS, *Vita Ambrosii*, XLVIII.
4 AMBROSE, *Epistula* LXXV [Maur.XX]; AUGUSTINE, *Confessions* IX.7.15; PAULINUS, *Vita Ambrosii*, XIII.
5 AMBROSE, *Epistula* LXXV ad Marcellinam [Maur.XX] 4-5.
6 EGERIA, *Itinerarium* XVII.8
7 AMBROSE, *De patriarchis* IX.38; *De virginibus* I.12.66.
8 *De sacramentis*, IV.6.28; V.4.25.

19

important consequences for the ministers of worship in a new requirement of absolute continence. Ambrose makes explicit reference to this in connection with more isolated and marginal districts where the 'ancient custom' was still followed: 'the sacrifice was offered with intervals between one celebration and another, when the people too could observe chastity for two or three days in order to approach the sacrifice in purity'.[1]

Other references to a Sunday in 386 when the basilicas were disputed show that the readings before the offering of the eucharist were three: OT, Pauline, Gospel.[2] The text does not give a precise chronological indication; if it is speaking of the same Sunday referred to in the *Epistula ad Marcellinam*, the gospel (Lk 19: entry into Jerusalem) could reflect the liturgical content of the day ('the lesson has been read not by our command, but purely for fitness; it is moreover well suited to the present circumstances'); the same can probaby be said for the Pauline epistle (Gal, approx. 2.16-3.14: justification by faith in Christ crucified); the OT pericope (I Kings 21: Naboth's vineyard) would seem to have been an *ad hoc* choice of the bishop.

De sacramentis states that before the eucharistic offering there comes the prayer for the people, for the rulers, and for others [3], while in *De mysteriis* Ambrose mentions the altar being prepared[4], and elsewhere deals with the 'mystic vessels'[5] and the presentation of the offerings at the altar by the faithful.[6] Here another passage from the *Commentary on Luke's gospel* is interesting: 'Oh, if only the angel would make himself present to us too, while we cense the altars and offer the sacrifice'[7]: the earliness of this testimony to incensation compared with all other contemporary witnesses has led to an interpretation in a metaphorical sense. Those departed who are termed *innoxi*, that is, comparable to the saints, can enjoy a special commemoration, according to *De obitu Valentiniano*: 'Who would forbid the naming of those who are free from sin?'[8]

Regarding his words on the eucharistic prayer (*sacrae orationis mysterium*[9], or *benedictio verborum caelestium*[10]) the central element for Ambrose is constituted by the words of Christ:

'This sacrament which you receive is produced by the words of Christ . . . the same Lord Jesus exclaimed, "This is my body". Before the blessing of the heavenly words the reality indicated is other, but after the consecration we understand it to be "body". He himself says that it is his blood. Before the consecration it is called something else, but after the consecration it is called blood'[11]

1 AMBROSE, *De officiis ministrorum* I.50.249.
2 AMBROSE, *Epistula LXXVa* [Maur.XXIa] [=*Contra Auxentium*]: 17.19.24-5.
3 *De sacramentis*, IV.4.14.
4 AMBROSE, *De mysteriis*, VIII.43.
5 AMBROSE, *De officiis ministrorum* II.28: 136, 143.
6 AMBROSE, *Expositio de ps.* CXVIII, prologue.
7 AMBROSE, *Expositio evangelii secundum Lucam* I.28.
8 AMBROSE, *De obitu Valentiniani*, 78.
9 AMBROSE, *De fide* IV.10.24
10 AMBROSE, *De mysteriis*, IX.54.
11 ibid. 52, 54.

This is clearly the same conception which is expressed in the *Explanatio psalmi XXXVIII* ('the body of Christ is offered, indeed the one who offers in us is Christ himself, whose word sanctifies the sacrifice which is offered')[1], a conception fully shared, and in fuller and more circumstantial terms, in the tractate *De sacramentis*:

> 'with which words is the consecration effected, and whose words are they? They are of the Lord Jesus. All the rest which is said before is said by the priest [i.e. the bishop] . . . when we reach the effecting of the venerable sacrament the priest no longer uses his own words, but those of Christ. It is therefore the word of Christ which effects this sacrament . . . Do you want to know how we consecrate with the heavenly words? Hear what these words are. The priest says, "Make this offering for us ratified, spiritual, pleasing, for it is the figure of the body and blood of our Lord Jesus Christ. He, on the eve of his passion . . ." Note: all those words are the evangelist's up to "take", both for the body and the blood. From then on they are the words of Christ . . . And note each detail. "He on the eve of his passion took the bread in his holy hands." Before it is consecrated it is bread; when the words of Christ are added, it is the body of Christ. Hear him in effect when he says, "Take of it and eat, all of you, this is in fact my body". Before Christ's words the chalice too is full of water and wine; after Christ's words have acted, the blood of Christ which redeemed the people is formed in it.'[2]

This sacramental understanding of the eucharistic prayer is not necessarily contradicted by the statement in *De Spiritu Sancto* that in the eucharistic offering there is an invocation of the Holy Spirit by 'the priests'[3]: the passage in question is a clear example of unacknowledged dependence on a Greek source.

The people respond to this mystery with their 'Amen'[4], which could be identified with the 'Amen' said at receiving communion[5], received by the faithful at the altar[6], which they approached probably singing Psalm XXII (XXIII) ('rightly do those who are filled with the spiritual food and drink say: You have prepared a table in my sight, and how splendid is your inebriating cup').[7]

The *De officiis ministrorum* also offers us precise ritual indications regarding the placing of the ministers—during the celebration—between the people and the 'orientated' altar: 'Not all can see the altar of the mysteries, as these are hidden by the levites so that those who should not see are not able to see'.[8]

1 AMBROSE, *Explanatio psalmi XXXVIII*, 25.
2 *De sacramentis*, IV.14,21, 22, 23.
3 AMBROSE, *De Spiritu Sancto*, III.18.16.112.
4 *De mysteriis* 54
5 cf.*De sacramentis* IV.25.
6 PAULINUS, *Vita Ambrosii* XLIV
7 AMBROSE, *De Helia et ieiunio*, X.34; cf. *De sacramentis*, V.3, 12-13.
8 AMBROSE, *De officiis ministrorum* I.50.251

As is well known, the *De sacramentis* is the most ancient attestation of the eucharistic canon of the Roman type.[1] The doubts which are raised about this text's authenticity, however, make it difficult to derive from it a scheme of what the eucharistic prayer was for Ambrose.

c. The ordering of lections and catechesis

Josef Schmitz, analysing the sermons of Ambrose, has carried out a thorough identification of the scriptural passages commented on by the bishop. As already noted, in some case these pericopes appear to be part of an already established system of readings, and the same applies to the related programme of catechesis, seen as part of the ecclesial tradition. The testimonies to this refer to the full cycle of weeks gravitating around Easter.

'We have heard and read that the Lord fasted, that he thirsted, that he wept': so speaks the *Expositio evangelii secundum Lucam*[2], with clear reference to the stories of the temptations, the Samaritan woman, Lazarus, pericopes proper (and not only in Milan) to the Sundays of Lent. On the reading of the story of the man born blind in this context, we find full documentation in the *Epistula LXVII* (Maur.: *LXXX*). It should be remembered that on the Sundays of Lent in Ambrose's time there were also the rites of preparation for initiation (this was so at least in the case of the *traditio Symboli*—the giving of the Creed).

The intense ferial catechesis for the *competentes*, of an essentially moral character in its first part, developed on the basis of Genesis and Proverbs.[3] This combination is also found in the Constantinopolitan scheme and in the Spanish; it appears also, but in the first three days of the Great Week, in the liturgy of Jerusalem of the early fifth century, according to the Armenian lectionaries. The reading of Proverbs in Lent is traceable to Jerusalem again in the archaic systematization of the second week of Lent, while the Genesis readings are found in Chrysostom's Antioch[4] and are still present in the lectionary of the East Syrian church.

In Milan at the time of Ambrose the reading of Job came in the first days of Holy Week[5], is earlier cited by Origen as for 'the days of the Passion'[6], and also, according to the Armenian evidence, appears in Jerusalem as readings spread out through Lent.

Less clear is the ritual setting of the Ambrosian references to Tobit.[7]

In Jerusalem Egeria reports that there is no more time in the Great Week for instructing the *competentes*, the celebrations and sermons being centred on the religious themes proper to those days.[8] A similar situation seems to be reflected

---

1   *De sacramentis*, IV: 5, 21 – 6, 28.
2   AMBROSE, *Expositio evangelii secundum Lucam*, VII, 182.
3   AMBROSE, *De mysteriis*, I, 1.
4   IOHANNES CHRYSISTINUS, *Homilia VII ad populum Antiochenum*.
5   AMBROSE: *Epistula LXXV* (Maur.: *XX*), 14; *De Iob*; Cf. ZENO Veronensis, *Tractatus*, I, XV : *De Iob*.
6   ORIGENES, *In Iob*, I, 1.
7   AMBROSE, *De Tobia*, I.1; *Exameron libri*, VI.4, 17.
8   EGERIA, *Itinerarium*, XLVI. 4.

in the *Exameron libri sex*, a collection of sermons given in Holy Week in Milan (perhaps in 387) and modelled on the homiletic exemplar of Basil. The idea—already present in Jewish usage—of the Pasch as a new Creation and the Christian concept of the the Resurrection constituting the eighth day, symbol of the eternal day without sunset, naturally led to a modelling of the *Hebdomada Authentica* (Holy Week) on the six primordial days. In this symbolic perspective the *Feria VI* (Friday) was presented as the day in which the redemption of humanity was linked to its creation.

In the homily of Book V Ambrose recalls that, on the day this sermon was given the reconciliation of penitents took place, the book of Jonah was read, and a gospel passage telling of Peter's denial, and, finally, the eucharist was celebrated. It is the same liturgical pattern set out, with reference to the year 386, in the *Epistula ad Marcellinam*:

'The following day, *according to custom*, the book of Jonah was read . . . this was the day in which the Lord gave himself up for us, the day in which in the church sinners are released from penitence.'[1]

There is no reference here to the eucharist, but its celebration at the reconciliation of penitents is definitely referred to in *De paenitentia*.[2]

As already noted, Ambrose speaks of the reading of Jonah as 'according to custom'. It does not seem too much to see this conformity to an already established order as involving more than the simple text of the reading.

It is almost certain that a precise programme of scripture readings lay behind the mystagogical catechesis of Easter Week.[3] We have noted above that the more uncertain *De sacramentis* nevertheless through its immediacy gives important evidence that for the preacher the course of readings followed an established scheme.[4]

d. Christian Initiation

Mystagogical preaching obviously offers much valuable information on how the initiation of believers was carried out in the last quarter of the fourth century in Milan. Besides this, we have further information from other writings.

We know that the catechumens, that is those who 'believed in the cross of the Lord Jesus and were signed in it'[5], were invited by the bishop to baptism on the day of Epiphany.[6] In order to take part in the catechesis and the preparatory rites of Lent they needed previously to 'give in their name', confirming it with

---

1 AMBROSE, *Epistula LXXV ad Marcellinam* (Maur.: XX), 25-26.
2 AMBROSE, *De paenitentia*, II.3, 18.
3 Cf. AMBROSE, *De mysteriis*: III.16; IV.22; VII.42; VIII.45.
4 *De sacramentis*: II.2, 3 ('*quid lectum est heri?*'); VI.2, 9 ('*ut lectum est nudius tertius*'); and note also VI.5, 26 (' We have taught within the limits of our abilities things which we perhaps have not *learnt*; we have given an exposition of them in the way that was possible for us').
5 AMBROSE, *De mysteriis*, IV.20.
6 AMBROSE, *Expositio evangelii secundum Lucam*, IV.76.

23

their own signature.[1] Augustine followed this procedure: 'When the time came in which the names were to be submitted, I left the country and returned to Milan.'[2]

The catechesis of the *competentes* in the contemporary Jerusalem of Egeria took place 'in the middle of the *ecclesia maior*' where the bishop's seat was set and there, sitting on the floor around him, the baptismal candidates gathered with their godfathers and godmothers and any other of the faithful who wanted; in Ambrose's Milan such catechesis had developed—as we have said—in connection with Genesis and Proverbs, and we have a more or less direct witness to it in *De Abraham*. The climax of this Milanese catechetical course was the *expositio Symboli* on the Sunday before Easter[3], something referred to also by the *Expositio evangelii secundum Lucam*.[4] As is well known, among the works attributed to Ambrose there is also a small tract dealing specifically with the *Symbol* (Creed).

The introduction to the actual baptismal rites themselves was the *aperitionis mysterium* (mystery of the opening); Ambrose reminds the neophytes of it, commenting on what he had said to them on the evening of Holy Saturday and the gesture which he at that time carried out:

'*Ephpheta, quod est Adaperire* [Ephphatha, which means 'Be opened'] was said, so that each of those who were about to attain to grace would recognize what was being required of them, and would remember what they had to reply; in the gospel Christ celebrated this sacred rite, as we read when he healed the deaf mute.'[5]

The reference is to Mk 7.32-35; but for reasons of convenience ('because it would not be appropriate for a woman') after touching the ears the bishop touched not the mouth but the nostrils of the candidate, recalling 2 Cor 2.15-16. No indication is given regarding the use of saliva, something that was present in the medieval rite in Milan; towards the middle of the sixth century in the area of the ecclesiastical province of Milan, a short mystagogical tract refers to the use of oil.[6]

The rite took place in front of the still-closed doors of the baptistery, because Ambrose continues: 'after these things the *sancta sanctorum* was opened for you and you entered into the sanctuary of regeneration'. Later Syrian, Gallic and Hispanic sources speak of the opening of Lent with a solemn rite of closing of the baptistery, only to be reopened during the Paschal rites.[7] While Ambrose's

1   AMBROSE, *De Helia et ieiunio*, XXI.79.
2   AUGUSTINE, *Confessiones*, IX.6.
3   AMBROSE, *Epistula LXXV ad Marcellinam* (Maur.: XX), 4-5.
4   AMBROSE, *Expositio evangelii secundum Lucam*, VI.107.
5   AMBROSE, *De mysteriis*, I.3-4.
6   Cf. *De sacramentis*, I.1, 2-3.
7   AMBROSE, *De mysteriis*, II.5; cf. *De sacramentis*: I.2, 4; IV.1, 2. The testimony of Severus of Antioch in A. BAUMSTARK, *Das Kirchenjahr in Antiocheia zwischen 512. und 518.*, "Römische Quartalschrift", X, pp 57 ff.; on the Hispanic and Gallican areas: PSEUDO-GERMANUS, *Epistula II*, PL, LXXII, c. ; PSEUDO-ILDEPHONSUS, *De cognitione baptismi*, CVII, PL, XCVI, c. 156.

De mysteriis moves on immediately to comment on the ritual dialogue in the baptistery with the renunciation of Satan, the *De sacramentis* reminds the neophyte that after entering the baptistery 'the levite came up to you, and the presbyter, and you were anointed as an athlete of Christ.'[1]

Turning to the west—'to see your adversary, whom you knew you had to renounce, saying it to his face' (the most authoritative textual traditions of *De mysteriis* exclude however the existence of the *sputatio* rite (spitting))—the candidate renounced 'the devil and all his works', as well as 'the world, its luxury and its pleasures', pronouncing the *Abrenuntio* in reply to *two* questions put to him/her.[2] After this rite the candidate could turn east: 'whoever renounces the devil turns to Christ and looks him directly in the face.'[3]

What was the scene at this point in the baptistery? Ambrose goes on to tell us:

'What did you see? The waters, of course, but not just them; there were the levites who carried out their service, and the high priest who asked the questions and who consecrated.'[4]

The *De sacramentis* specifies that the *sacerdos* stood *supra fontem* (over the font)[5], and that arrangement is well identifiable on archaeological grounds. The first baptistery of the *basilica vetus*, where Ambrose himself probaly received Christian initiation, originally provided for the bishop to stand on a small platform on the north side of the basin; only at a second stage was the basin itself conformed to the model of Ambrose's baptistery annexed to the *basilica nova*, the position of the bishop being transferred to the east. This is the scheme presupposed by *De mysteriis*.

The blessing of the water is commented on in the mystagogical catechesis of Ambrose, with biblical images and references which we find condensed in a page of the *Expositio evangelii secundum Lucam*[6], where we find remarkable verbal correspondences with the blessing-formula later attested in the Ambrosian liturgical books.

After the bishop's prayer over the waters, the candidates went down into the font, and here, replying to a triple interrogation, they affirmed their trinitarian profession of faith, it being accompanied by a triple immersion. The summary description in *De mysteriis*[7] becomes more comprehensible in the light of what is expounded in the *De sacramentis*:

'You came to the font, you went down into it, you turned to the high priest; in the font you saw the levites and the presbyter ... You were

---

1   *De sacramentis*, I.2, 4.
2   AMBROSE, *De mysteriis*, II.5, 7; cf. *De sacramentis*, I.2, 5; echoes in AMBROSE, *De fuga saeculi*: VIII.45, IX.57; the formula '*Abrenuntio tibi diabole*' in *Hexameron*, I.4, 14, reflects the Greek literary model used and translated by Ambrose.
3   AMBROSE, *De mysteriis*, II.7.
4   AMBROSE, *De mysteriis*, III.8.
5   *De sacramentis*, I.3, 9.
6   AMBROSE, *De mysteriis*, III.9-V.27; cf. *De sacramentis*, I.4, 11 – II.5, 15. AMBROSE, *Expositio evangelii secundum Lucam*, X.48.
7   AMBROSE, *De mysteriis*, V.28.

asked, "Do you believe in God the Father omnipotent?". You replied, "I believe", and you were immersed, that is you were buried. Again you were asked, "Do you believe in our Lord Jesus Christ and his cross?". You said, "I believe" and you were immersed. In this you were buried with Christ, and whoever is buried with Christ rises with Christ. For the third time you were asked: "Do you believe also in the Holy Spirit?". You said. "I believe"; you were immersed the third time.'[1]

Having entered the font from the west, the candidate approached the bishop to the east ('You went up to the priest'[2]). Then there came the great chrismation; 'we are all in fact anointed by the grace of the Spirit for the kingdom of God and the priesthood'[3]; the De Sacramentis specifies that the *myrum* was poured on the head and it gives us the formula used by the 'high priest'[4]: it is substantially the formula later set in the liturgical books of both Rome and Milan. We should note the fundamental importance of this anointing with chrism in the sacramental economy. Summing up a constant patristic tradition, which in the west is testified to by Tertullian[5]; the Spaniard Isidore, following the nexus— *Christus-chrisma-Christianus*, wrote:

'To kings and priests the mystic unction which was a figure of Christ was given only once. In fact the name itself derives from the chrism. But after the heavenly and mystical balsam had been poured out by God the Father onto our Lord, no longer just pontifexes and kings, but the whole church—that is, the members of the eternal king and priest—is consecrated with the anointing of chrism. As we are a priestly and royal race, we are therefore anointed after the bath, so as to be designated with the name of Christ.'[6]

At Milan (but also in Gaul) in the time of Ambrose and until the middle ages, there was at this point a further sacramental rite:

'You came up out of the font. Remember the reading of the gospel (John 13.4-11). In fact in the gospel our Lord Jesus Christ washed the feet of his disciples. When he came to Simon Peter, Peter said: "You will never wash my feet". He did not perceive the mystery.'[7]

In *De sacramentis* we find a more detailed description of this moment in the celebration, besides its well-known apologia in response to quarrels in the Roman church which did not know of this rite:

'The priest, wrapped in a cloth—in effect, although the rite was also carried out by presbyters, it was nevertheless the high priest who launched the ministerial act—the high priest, as I said, girded in a cloth washed your feet. What is this mystery? . . . There are some who say that it does not need to be done within the mysteries, not in baptism, not

1 De sacramentis. II.6, 16: 7, 20.
2 AMBROSE. De mysteriis, VI.29.
3 AMBROSE. De mysteriis, VI.30.
4 De sacramentis. II.7, 24.
5 TERTULLIAN. Apologeticum, III.5.
6 ISIDORUS Hispalensis. De ecclesiasticis officiis, II.26, 1-2.
7 AMBROSE. De mysteriis. VI.31.

in regeneration, but in connection with the duty to wash the feet of guests. But the one is a gesture of humility, the other the act of sanctification. Attend and hear that we are dealing with a mystery and with sanctification: "If I do not wash your feet, you have no part in me".'[1] After this came the giving of white garments.[2] Ambrose shows an unusual awareness of the profound meaning of this rite. The Pauline idea of the nuptial bath (Eph 5.26) and the gospel image of the wedding garment (Mt 22.11), while not explicitly cited, are presupposed in his commentary, developed through abundant reference to the Song of Songs:

'Seeing these garments the daughters of Zion, overcome with amazement, say: "Who is she who ascends all white?" She was black—how has she suddenly become all white? . . . and Christ, seeing his church in white robes . . . says: "Behold you are lovely, my friend, behold you are lovely, your eyes are as doves" . . . "Put me as a seal on your heart" so that your faith may shine resplendent in an oath fully carried out. . . May no persecution diminish your affection, which neither the great waters can undo, nor rivers overrun.'[3]

Proceeding further, *De mysteriis* says in connection with the next ritual moment: 'Remember therefore that you have received the seal of the Spirit: Spirit of wisdom and understanding, Spirit of counsel and strength, Spirit of knowledge and devotion, Spirit of holy fear; and guard that which you have received. God the Father has signed you, Christ the Lord has confirmed you and given you the Spirit as a pledge in your heart.'[4]

These words, as in the text of the *De Spiritu Sancto* which referes to the *Spiritale signaculum*[5], make no reference at all to any second chrismation; even on the basis of Milanese testimonies, then, the second anointing appears to be a unique practice peculiar to the Roman church.

'Having been made clean by the lavacrum and enriched by these signs the people go to the altar of Christ saying: Shall I go in to the altar of God?'[6] Initiation therefore reached its culmination with this night-time procession, which a little work not written by Ambrose—the *De lapsu virginis* (V.19)—says is marked by the *lumina neophytorum splendida* (shining light of the neophytes).[7] 'Introibo ad altare Dei' (I will go to the altar of God): in effect the destination of the neophytes was the altar in the sanctuary. This is the context of Paulinus' narrative which tells how, at the death of Ambrose on Holy Saturday 397,

'the baptized children coming from the font saw him, some saying he was sitting on his *cathedra*, others pointing in order to show their parents as he ascended the podium.'[8]

1   *De sacramentis*, III.1: 4, 5; cf. *De virginitate*, X.57; for the symbolic interpretation referring to the serpent's threat to the heel—also to be found in *De sacramentis*, III.1, 7—cf. *Explanatio psalmi XLVIII*.8.
2   AMBROSE, *De mysteriis*, VII.35; *Expositio evangelii secundum Lucam*, V.25.
3   AMBROSE, *De mysteriis*, VII.34-41.
4   AMBROSE, *De mysteriis*, VII.42; Cf. *De sacramentis*, III.2, 8-10.
5   AMBROSE, *De Spiritu Sancto*, I.6, 71-72.
6   AMBROSE, *De mysteriis*, VIII.43; cf. *De sacramentis*: III.2, 11; IV.2, 5-7.
7   *De lapsu virginis*, V.19.
8   PAULINUS, *Vita Ambrosii*, XLVIII.1.

The neophytes were placed in the sanctuary during the whole octave, taking part in the eucharist and hearing the mystagogical catechesis which, *only after initiation had taken place*, explained to them the mysteries they had experienced on the night of Easter. This was the principle of sacramental teaching in the church of the Fathers, and something Ambrose in Milan conformed to as well, in the conviction that

> 'the light itself of the mysteries is better transfused in those who are surprised when they receive it than if they had had some word beforehand.'[1]

e. Gradations of ministry; ordination

As is known, in the personal case of Ambrose in 374, initiation took place on the anomalous date of 30 November and the mystagogical octave became also the initiation to the ministry:

'It is handed on that once he had been baptized, he completed all the ecclesiastical offices and on the eighth day [7 December], to the great satisfaction and joy of all, was ordained bishop.'[2] This procedure, contrary to the canons, could explain the expression in *De officiis ministrorum*: 'I began to teach you what I myself had not yet learnt.'[3]

A passage in *De officiis ministrorum* alludes to the various ministries: 'One is good at reading the lesson, another better with the psalm, another still is more diligent in exorcizing those vexed by evil spirits, and another yet again is thought best in the service of holy things.' It was at all events the bishop's responsibility to evaluate the situation and 'assign to each the office that suited.'[4]

The cemetery area near the basilica of St Eustorgius has preserved for us the sepulchral inscription of an exorcist working in the times of Ambrose: Victurinus, laid to rest there on 11 November 377 (cf. also the exorcist Saturus, married to Nonnita and buried in the cemetery *ad martyres*[5]).

The first grade of church ministry was that of lector, which could be taken even in youth. In the *De excessu fratris* Ambrose refers to a reading just completed by a 'little reader'[6], and this could throw light on the observation in the *Expositio evangelii secundum Lucam*, whereby the Lord, reading the scriptures in the synagogue at Capernaum, did it in such a manner that 'the office of lector was not brought into disrepute.'[7]

There is repeated mention in the mystagogical catechesis of the higher ministers of the hierarchy: deacon, presbyter, bishop; in regard to this Ambrose

---

1 AMBROSE, *De mysteriis*, I.2. On the Sunday after Easter, after being introduced with full consciousness into the mysteric life of the church through mystagogical catechesis, the baptized were allowed to carry to the altar their own gifts for the eucharistic sacrifice, as was the custom for the faithful to do: AMBROSE, *Expositio de Psalmo CXVIII*, Prologus, 2.
2 PAULINUS, *Vita Ambrosii*, IX.
3 AMBROSE, *De officiis ministrorum*, I.1, 4; Cf. *De sacramentis*, VI.5, 26
4 AMBROSE, *De officiis ministrorum*, I.44, 216.
5 CIL, V.6252.
6 AMBROSE, *De excessu fratris*, I.6.
7 AMBROSE, *Expositio evangelii secundum Lucam*, IV.45; with reference to *Lk* 4.16.

advises the neophyte 'not to consider their physical appearance, but the grace of their ministries.'[1]

Reception into the presbyteral order is expressly mentioned in a letter to the priest Orontianus, to whom Ambrose says:

'remember the grace of God and the office which you have received through the imposition of my hands, so that even in this hierarchical grade you may show faith and commitment, as you did before in the holy diaconate (*ministerio*), and may await the recompense of the Lord Jesus.'[2]

The inscription concerning the priest Probus goes back to the episcopate of Ambrose's predecessor Auxentius: he lived for thirty years with his wife Virginia and died an octogenarian in 368 after 25 years in the clergy, into which he had been received in the time of bishop Protasius.[3]

With regard to episcopal ministry, Ambrose refers to it as a foundational and structural element of the church: 'Where is the church if not where the staff and the grace of the episcopate flourish?'[4] In regard to ordination to this ministry in particular Ambrose's awareness of the Metropolitan's responsibilities is very clear. To bishop Felix he writes that the Lord's satisfaction with his ministry as first bishop of Como

'will for me be a very sweet fruit, as it will confirm my judgement of you, and the ordination you have received through the imposition of my hands will not be censured, and the benediction conferred on you in the name of the Lord Jesus.'[5]

Writing to the church at Vercelli which was waiting to receive a bishop, he speaks of the sacerdotal vesting of Eleazar, son of Aaron, not by the people but by Moses alone, to show that 'it must be the priest [*sacerdos*] who consecrates the priest.'[6] His lack of reserve towards the non-canonical practice of the Thessalonian Acolius in designating his successor seems to follow in this line of thinking[7], a practice which he himself in some fashion followed when before his death he expressed his preference for the name of Simplicianus, who in fact did indeed follow him.[8] This did not mean that Ambrose did not recognize the role of the people and their fellow citizens too in ordination: of Acolius he said that he had been requested for the high priesthood by the peoples of Macedonia and had been elected by the bishops[9]; he himself together with his suffragans proceeded to the ordination of Gaudentius of Brescia, who called him *communis pater*[10]; and

---

1 AMBROSE, *De mysteriis*, II.6; Cf. *De sacramentis*, I.2, 7; similarly AMBROSE, *De officiis ministrorum*, II.24, 122.
2 AMBROSE, *Epistula* [Maur.: LXX], 25.
3 *Milano capitale dell'Impero romano, 286-402. Catalogo della Mostra* [Exhibition catalogue], Milan, Palazzo Reale, 24 January-22 April 1990, ed. G. SENA CHIESA, Milan, 1990, p 113a (No. 2a 18a); on Victurinus the exorcist; p 116a-?????????.
4 AMBROSE, *De Isaac et anima*, VIII.64.
5 AMBROSE, *Epistula V* (Maur.: IV), 6.
6 AMBROSE, *Epistula e. c. XIV* (Maur.: LXIII), 59.
7 AMBROSE, *Epistula LI* (Maur.: XV), 9.
8 PAULINUS, *Vita Ambrosii*, XLVI.1.
9 AMBROSE, *Epistula LI* (Maur.: XV), 12.
10 GAUDENTIUS Brixiensis, *Tractatus XVI*.

as far as regards the faithful of Milan, he had no doubt about having recourse to them, calling them sons/daughters [translator's note—Italian:*figli*], but also parents: 'you have in fact been parents to me, who have passed on to me the priesthood.'[1] It is in the context of the profound bond between the bishop and the whole body of the church that the annual celebration of the ordination anniversary has to be seen, the *dies natalis* of the episcopate, which he remembers in the case of the other bishops[2] and which he himself celebrated with his own faithful, by whom he had been elected.[3]

f. Rites of matrimony and consecrated virginity

Besides the plentiful treatment of virginity, often interwoven with the theme of marriage, the writings of Ambrose give us some interesting information on the rituals for entering on these states of life. The rite for virgins was inspired, in no small measure, by nuptial rites, and for Christians it was also connected with the realities of human living in those times and their related symbolic language.

Strictly understood in the light of the principle that '*non defloratio virginitatis facit coniugium, sed pactio coniugalis*'[4] (it is not the defloration of virginity that makes the marriage, but the conjugal pact), and to be celebrated only among Christians already orthodox and initiated into the divine mysteries[5], marriage was preceded by nuptials, i.e. the ceremony of engagement in which ritual elements were the ring, sign of faithfulness and its pledge[6], and the kiss— established in Constantine's legislation—a ratification of the promised fidelity, and pledge of the wedding.[8]

The characteristic feature of the the nuptial rite was the donning of the bridal veil.[9] This is the ceremony which for Ambrose sums up the whole rite and which in his church appears to have been presided over by the bishop himself ('marriage has to be sanctified by episcopal veiling and by the blessing'): a usage which he impresses on the bishops of his province.[10]

The *velatio* (veiling) of 'holy virgins' apparently derived from nuptial symbolism, and had its own prayer of blessing by the bishop.[11] The information on this in *De lapsu virginis* cannot be taken into account as it does not belong to Ambrose's writings; but we can be sure that Ambrose celebrated this rite at

1   AMBROSE, *Expositio evangelii secundum Lucam*, VIII.73.
2   AMBROSE, *Epistula V* (Maur.: *IV*), 1-3.
3   AMBROSE, *Expositio evangelii secundum Lucam*, VIII.73ff.
4   AMBROSE, *De institutione virginis*, VI.41.
5   AMBROSE, *De Abraham*, I.9, 84; a difficult situation arose if only one of the couple were converted: *Expositio evangelii secundum Lucam*, VIII.3.
6   AMBROSE, *Expositio evangelii secundum Lucam*, VII.21; *De paenitentia*, II.3, 18.
7   *Codex Theodosianus*, III.5, 6.
8   AMBROSE, *Explanatio psalmi XXXIX.*17; *Epistula* (Maur.: *XLI*).18.
9   AMBROSE: *De virginitate*, V.26; *Exhortatio virginitatis*, VI.34.
10 AMBROSE, *Epistula LXII* (Maur.: *XIX*), 7.
11 AMBROSE, *Epistula LVI* (Maur.: *V*), 1; Cf. *De virginibus*, I.11, 65; *De institutione virginis*, XVII.108.

Easter[1] and on the feast of the apostles Peter and Paul[2], and perhaps Christmas.[3] In *De virginibus*, while recalling to his sister Marcellina the words of Pope Liberius in the Vatican basilica when Marcellina herself had received the veil, he states that it took place on the Lord's Nativity[4]; as Ambrose associates that day not only with Mary's motherhood but also with the story of Cana and the multiplication of the loaves, it has been thought that he was referring to a single epiphanic feast of the Incarnation (about a century after Pope Gelasius had set Easter week, Epiphany and feasts of the apostles for the *velatio*[5]).

Still in *De virginibus*, there is mention of a *mutatio vestis* (change of robes) for Marcellina, which can be explained as the putting on—and not, it seems, in a purely symbolic sense—of that *stola*[6] which elsewhere Ambrose describes as 'spiritual dress and nuptial robe.'[7] For monks as well there seems most certainly to have been a special dress.[8]

g. Penitence

'The bishop's food is the remission of sins'[9]: this statement by the Milanese bishop expresses well the prominent position of the administration of penitence in his ministry—it was not fortuitous that he devoted a whole treatise to it. In its public and episcopal form penitence only concerned the 'most grave sins', and could not, according to the bishop of Milan, be repeated: 'as baptism is one, so is penitence one.'[10] The remission of minor sins was left to the doing of good works: 'charity in fact hides error and covers a multitude of sins.'[11]

Paulinus give us a lively vignette of St Ambrose administering penitence, a picture confirmed in Ambrose's own writings:

'Every time someone confessed their sins to him in order to receive penance, he wept in such a way that it made the other begin to weep; for he saw himself to be fallen with all who had fallen. He never spoke with anyone about the sins which were confessed to him, but only with God, with whom he interceded; in this way he left a good example to the bishops who followed him, that they might be intercessors to God rather than accusers to men.'[12]

---

1   AMBROSE. *Exhortatio virginitatis*, VII.42.
2   AMBROSE. *De virginitate*, XIX.24-26.
3   Cf.the insistence on the virginal motherhood of Mary in *De institutione virginis*: XII-XIII; XVII.104-110
4   AMBROSE. *De virginibus*, III.1,1.
5   GELASIUS I Romanus. *Epistula XIV ad universus episcopos per Lucaniaem, Brutus et Silician constitutus*, 12.
6   AMBROSE. *De institutione virginis*, XVI: 100, 102.
7   AMBROSE. *Expositio evangelii secundum Lucam*, VII.231.
8   AMBROSE. *Epistula* (Maur.: LVIII), 3; *Epistula LI* (Maur.: XV): 9, 12.
9   AMBROSE. *Epistula III* (Maur.: LXVII), 11.
10 AMBROSE. *De paenitentia*, II.10, 95.
11 AMBROSE: *Apologia prophetae David*, I.9, 50; *Explanatio psalmi XLIII*.47.
12 PAULINUS. *Vita Ambrosii*, XXXIX.1-2; Cf. AMBROSE. *De paenitentia*, II.8, 73.

After the confession the sinner was placed in a state of penitence, perhaps according to a variety of categories and grades which however remain unknown to us.[1] Prayer, tears, requests to the rest of the faithful for intercession, were the attitudes proper to penitents[2] until they were reconciled. Reconciliation was given annually on Maundy Thursday as we have said, and was followed that same day with participation in the eucharist.[3] A special rite was provided, accompanied by an absolution formula:

'In the remission of sins what human beings make manifest is their ministry, not any right they might claim on the basis of some power of their own; in fact they do not remit sins in their own name, but in the name of the Father and of the Son and of the Holy Spirit. They pray and the Divinity grants.'[4]

Not even the emperor was exempted by Ambrose from this discipline; in the autumn of 390, after the massacre of Thessalonica, he wrote to Theodosius: 'If you were to attend, I would not dare to offer the sacrifice.'[5] Theodosius 'laid aside all insignia of imperial power and wept publicly in the church for his own sin to which he had been led by the deceit of others; with sighs and tears he asked for pardon; he the emperor did not even blush to carry out a public penance which makes private citizens shamefaced.'[6] In this case, according to Theodoret, reconciliation was given at Christmas.[7]

h. Rituals for illness and mourning

Imposition of hands on the sick and the related blessing must have been commonly practised in the church of St Ambrose, given his comments while discussing its use among the Novatianists.[8]

More circumstantial are references to rites and memorials for departed believers. While Paulinus speaks in connection with Ambrose of the eucharistic viaticum at the moment of passing[9], the pages written by Ambrose himself about his brother Satirus inform us that his remains were brought into church and there Ambrose celebrated the eucharist.[10] Afterwards, before interment, there was the final threefold *vale* (farewell) and the kiss according to eastern fashion.[11]

---

1 AMBROSE, *De paenitentia*, II.7, 54.
2 AMBROSE, *De paenitentia*: I.16, 90-91; II.9, 81.
3 AMBROSE: *Epistula LXXVI* (Maur.: *XX*), 25-26; *Hexameron*, V.24, 90-91; *De paenitentia*, II.3, 18.
4 AMBROSE, *De Spiritu Sancto*, III.18, 139.
5 AMBROSE, *Epistula e. c. XI* (Maur.: *LI*), 11.
6 AMBROSE, *De obitu Theodosii*, 34.
7 THEODORETUS, *Historia Ecclesiastica*, V.17-18.
8 AMBROSE, *De paenitentia*, I.8, 26.
9 PAULINUS, *Vita Ambrosii*, XLVII.3; on the similar Roman practice: Gerontius, *Vita Melaniae*; Cf. subsequently also the *Statuta Ecclesiae Antiqua*, can. 20.
10 AMBROSE, *De excessu fratris*, I.80; the same seems to have been done for Ambrose himself: Paulinus, *Vita Ambrosii*, XLVIII.1.
11 AMBROSE, *De excessu fratris*, I.78.

There was then a special commemoration on the seventh day after death, 'which is the day symbolizing eternal rest'[1], and (for Theodosius) on the fortieth[2], as well as on the annual commemoration.[3] But Ambrose also knows the custom of celebrating the third and thirtieth day.[4] The bishop urges as well that the souls of the departed should be committed to God by the *oblationes* of their loved ones.[5]

i. Cult of the saints

In Ambrose's works we also find hints of the ancient Milanese sanctoral: the *natalis* (heavenly 'birthday') of the martyr Sebastian is mentioned[6], and the feast of Peter and Paul with its solemn vigil[7], as well as the Martyr Agnes.[8] To the veneration at the tomb of the martyrs Felix, Nabor and Victor would have been added the cult of the martyrs discovered by Ambrose: Protasius and Gervasius[9] (whose discovery was celebrated each year not only in Milan but also in Africa[10]), Vitale and Agricola[11], Nazarius and Celsus.[12]

To Ambrose on the other hand is owed the definitive prohibition of ritual banquets of porridge, bread and wine[13] at the tombs of martyrs, a widespread practice in Rome and Africa.[14]

j. Dedication of churches

Closely connected to the cult of martyrs and their relics were the dedications of churches carried out by Ambrose in Milan, as well as the foundation in Florence of a basilica to which he gave the relics of the martyrs Vitale and Agricola, discovered shortly before in Bologna.

The dedication in Milan of the 'Roman' basilica, that is the basilica of the Apostles, which was on the road leading to Rome, took place in May 386, and was marked by the placing there of the relics of saints John, Andrew and Thomas. More details are forthcoming about the basilica *ad martyres*, i.e. the 'Ambrosian' basilica, at whose dedication the relics of the martyrs Gervasius and Protasius

---

1 AMBROSE, *De excessu fratris*, II.2.
2 AMBROSE, *De obitu Theodosii*, 3.
3 AMBROSE, *De excessu fratris*, II.5.
4 AMBROSE, *De obitu Theodosii*, 3. While the third, seventh and thirtieth were the commemorative days in use at Rome and in Africa, the third, ninth and fortieth, as well as the anniversary, had found sanction in the east, also in the *Apostolic Constitutions*, VIII.42.
5 AMBROSE, *Epistula VIII* (Maur.: *XXXIX*), 4.
6 AMBROSE, *Expositio de psalmo CXVIII*, XX.44.
7 AMBROSE, *De virginitate*, XIX.125: concerning the interpretation of *II Cor* 11.29, Paul's apology; and citation of *Lk* 5.5: calling of Peter. On the homily given on this day in Milan by Gaudentius of Brescia: GAUDENTIUS Brixiensis, *Tractatus XX*.
8 AMBROSE, *De virginibus*, I.2, 5.
9 PAULINUS, *Vita Ambrosii*, XIV; AMBROSE, *Epistula LXXVII* (Maur.: *XXII*), 2 ff.; AUGUSTINE, *Confessions*, IX.7.
10 AMBROSE, *Expositio de psalmo CXVIII*, VI.16; AUGUSTINE, *Sermo CCLXXXVI*, 5.
11 PAULINUS, *Vita Ambrosii* IX; AMBROSE, *Exhortatio virginitatis*, I.
12 PAULINUS, *Vita Ambrosii*, XXXII-XXXIII.
13 AUGUSTINE, *Confessions*, VI.22; AMBROSE, *De Helia et ieiunio*, XVII.62.
14 AUGUSTINE: *Epistula XXIX*.10; *Epistula XXII*.3.

were placed in a small church nearby (*Basilica Faustae*), a vigil was held there through the night, and the next day they were solemnly translated and deposited below the altar of the Ambrosian basilica[1]: this was a liturgical pattern widely shared and variously developed subsequently in the Christian *oikumene*.

Ambrose is said to have died on Holy Saturday (4 April) 397. Five years later the imperial court left Milan, and very difficult times followed. Church life underwent important changes, but one constant element seems to have been the recourse to the great bishop's authority. The status of a paradigm accorded to Ambrose in late antique Milan involved, as we have already seen, the area of doctrine; but discipline and forms of worship were also in some ways marked by his recognized status as exemplar. In fact subsequent history shows a dynamic evolution of ritual arrangements and customs present in Milan at the time of Ambrose, but by the same token a tenacious continuity in the structures and elements of that ancient inheritance. This was not born with Ambrose; there flowed into it a patrimony—not only of buildings—passed on to him by his predecessors, among whom he cites Mirocles, Eustorgius and Dionysius.[2] Nevertheless, after Ambrose these things were connected as a whole with his person and seen as an essential part of his heritage, and so this became the *Ambrosianum Mysterium*.

---

1   PAULINUS, *Vita Ambrosii*, XIV; AMBROSE, *Epistula LXXVII* (Maur.: *XXII*), 1 ff.; AUGUSTINE, *Confessions*, IX.7.
2   AMBROSE, *Epistula LXXVa* (Maur.: *XXIa*) [= *Sermo contra Auxentium*], 17-18.

Bibliographical note

On Constantinian legislation affecting more or less directly Christian liturgical practice and ministers: J.HE GAUDEMET, *La législation religieuse de Constantin*, 'Revue d'histoire de l'Église de France', XXXIII (1972), pp 25-61. On Constantine's project for the sanctuary at Jerusalem, which was dedicated in 335: V. CORBO, *Il Santo Sepolcro di Gerusalemme*, 3 vols., Jerusalem 1982. There is a long tradition of studies of the liturgical model at Jerusalem and its influence in the Christian *oikumene*; the following are only a selection from an enormous body of historiography: D. BALDI, *La liturgia di Gerusalemme*, Jerusalem 1952; G. KRETSCHMAR, *Die frühe Geschichte der Jerusalemer Liturgie*, 'Jahrbuch für Liturgik und Hymnologie', II (1956), pp 22-46; C. GARCIA DEL VALE, *Jerusalém. Un siglo de oro de la vida liturgica*, Madrid 1968; H. LEEB, *Die Gesänge im Gemeindegottesdienst von Jerusalem (vom 5. bis. 8. Jahrhundert)*, Vienna 1970; A. TARBY, *La prière eucharistique de l'Église de Jérusalem*, Paris 1972; with specific reference to the cycle of scripture readings through the year, which stabilized at the beginning of the fifth century: A. RENOUX, *Le codex Arménien Jérusalem 121*, I: *Introduction. Aux origines de la liturgie hiérosolimitane. Lumières nouvelles*, Turnhout 1969 (Patrologia Orientalis, XXXV, 1, N° 163); II: *Édition comparée du texte et de deux autres manuscrits*, Turnhout 1971 (Patrologia Orientalis, XXXVI, 2, N° 168).

On the first buildings for Christian worship in Roman Milan: M. MIRABELLA ROBERTI, *Milano romana*, Milan 1984; *Il Millennio ambrosiano*, I: *Milano, una capitale da Ambrogio ai Carolingi*, ed. C. BERTELLI, Milan 1988; *Milano capitale dell'Impero romano. 286-402. Catalogo della Mostra. Milano, Palazzo Reale, 24 gennaio – 22 aprile 1990*, ed. G. SENA CHIESA, Milan 1990; *Milano e la sua memoria. Milano e la tradizione di sant'Ambrogio. Catalogo della Mostra. Museo Diocesano ai Chiostri di Sant'Eustorgio, Milano, 3 aprile – 8 giugno 1997*, ed. M. RIZZI, Milan 1997. On the episcopal complex in particular and its two places of worship: A. PRACCHI, *La cattedrale antica di Milano. Il problema delle chiese doppie fra tarda antichità e medioevo*, Rome-Bari 1996 (Università Laterza. Architettura, V); S. LUSUARDI SIENA, *Il complesso episcopale di Milano: riconsiderazione della testimonianza ambrosiana nella* Epistola ad sororem, in *Les Églises doubles et les familles d'églises*: 'Antiquité tardive', IV (1996), pp 124-129; particularly on the baptistery, EADEM, *Il complesso episcopale di Milano e il battesimo di Agostino: un punto di vista archeologico*, 'Collectanea Augustiniana', Villanova University, IV (1998). On palaeo-Christian inscriptions in Milan see the corresponding volume, *Mediolanum*, of the *Inscriptiones Christianae Italiae*, ed. G. CUSCITO.

On the various western liturgical traditions, including the Milanese, a **common Roman origin** for them was claimed by PROBST (*Liturgie des vierten Jahrhunderts und deren Reform*, Münster 1893; *Die abendländische Messe vom fünften bis zum achten Jahrhundert*, Münster 1896), CERIANI (*Notitia Liturgiae Ambrosianae*, Mediolani 1895), MAGISTRETTI (*Cenni sul Rito Ambrosiano*, Milan 1895), CAGIN (in *Paléographie Musicale*, V, 1896), MAGANI (*L'antica liturgia romana*, I, Milan 1897), MERCATI (*Sull'origine della liturgia gallicana*, in *Antiche reliquie liturgiche ambrosiane e romane*, Vatican City, 1902 [Studi e Testi, VII]), CABROL (*Les origines liturgiques*, Paris 1906, pp 353 ff.), MORIN (*Depuis quand un Canon fixe à Milan? Restes de ce qu'il a remplacé*, 'Revue Bénédictine', [1939], pp 89-93), DIX (*The Shape of the Liturgy*, Glasgow 1945, chap. V), GRIFFE (*Aux origines de la liturgie gallicane*, 'Bulletin de littérature ecclésiastique', [1951], pp 17-43), JUNGMANN (*La liturgie de l'Église romaine*, Paris 1957). For his part DUCHESNE (*Origines du culte chrétien*, Paris, chap. III) had earlier evolved a hypothesis that the Gallican and Hispanic liturgical traditions came from a common root, whose main ecclesiastical centre was Milan; the same line was followed by LEJAY (*Rit romain et rit gallican*, 'Revue d'histoire et de littérature religieuses', [1897], pp 93-96), and others followed on, including BAUMSTARK (*Liturgia romana e liturgia dell'Esarcato. Il Rito detto in seguito Patriarchino e le origini del* Canon Missae *romano*, Rome 1904, chap. IV), up until GAMBER (*I più antichi libri liturgici dell'Alta Italia. Descrizione dei manoscritti e frammenti del 550-750*, 'Rivista di Storia della Chiesa in Italia', XV (1961), pp 71-81; *Zur ältesten Liturgie von Mailand*, "Ephemerides Liturgurgicae", [1963], pp 391-395). In fact recent research by Judith FREI on the Milanese *Missal of St Simplicianus* has identified for the ferial eucharistic liturgy in Lent an archaic euchological foundation for which we must presuppose a pre-Carolingian form of celebration of an evolved Gallican type (*Das ambrosianische Sakramentar D 3-3 aus dem mailändischen Metropolitankapitel*, Münster 1974).

The presence of a **eucharistic prayer of Roman type** in the Milanese church at least from the time of Ambrose depends on the witness of *De sacramentis*. However the Ambrosian and Milanese origin of this short mystagogical treatise, put in doubt by Murini, has been decisively refuted in this century by Baumstark and Gamber cited above (on the more general opinion in favour of its authenticity: CH. MOHRMANN, *Observations sur le 'De Sacramentis' et le 'De Mysteris' de saint Ambroise*, in *Ambrosius Episcopus* [cit.], I, Milan 1976, pp 103-123); it is worth noting that in the recent *Thesaurus Sancti Ambrosii*, Turnhout 1994 (CC, ThesPL) and the *CETEDOC Library of Christian Latin Texts* (1963), prepared under the guidance of Hervé Savon, this treatise has been placed among the *dubia* (cf. H. SAVON, *Ambroise prédicateur*, in *La Prèdication* [= 'Connaissance des Pères de l'Église', fsc. LXXIV, juin 1999], pp 33-34). This scepticism is shared also by the present author, who cannot however avoid noting in the text some unique statements of an autobiographical character, such as the tiring of the voice: (I.6. 24; cf. the no less disputed *Apologia David altera*, V.28, and the testimony of Augustine: *Confessions*, VI.3.3; this seems to be confirmed by the pathological picture revealed by analysis of the relics: G. JUDICA CORDIGLIA, *La malattia e la morte di s. Ambrogio*, 'La Scuola Cattolica', [1941]), as well as the statement by the preacher on the inadequacy of his catechetical formation (VI.5.26; cf. *De officiis ministrorum*, I.1.4).

On the forms of worship attested in Ambrose's writings a rich tradition of studies has grwon up: here we cannot fail to note, for its significance for Ambrosian historiography (notwithstanding its obvious limitations), the volume by M. MAGISTRETTI, *La liturgia della Chiesa milanese nel secolo IV*, which appeared in Milan 100 years ago; nearer to our time are the works of A. PAREDI (*La liturgia di sant'Ambrogio*, in *Sant'Ambrogio nel XVI centenario della nascita*, Milan 1940, pp 69-157), H. LEEB (*Die Psalmodie bei Ambrosius*, Vienna 1967 [Wiener Beiträge zur Theologie, XVIII]), J. SCHMITZ (*Gottesdienst im altchristlichen Mailand. Eine liturgiewissenschaftliche Untersuchung über Initiation und Meßfeier während des Jahres zur Zeit des Bischofs Ambrosius. †397*, Köln-Bonn 1975 [Theophaneia, XXV]), as well as the recent researches of A. FRANZ (*Die Tagzeitenliturgie der Mailänder Kirche im 4. Jahrhundert*, 'Archiv für Liturgiewissenschaft', XXXIV [1992], pp 23-83; *Ambrosius der Dichter*, 'Archiv für Liturgiewissenschaft', XXXV [1993/94], pp 140-149, with reference to *Ambroise de Milan, Hymnes. Texte établi, traduit et annoté sous la direction de Jacques Fontaine*, PARIS 1992).

On the mysterical aspect (that is, in reference ot the experience of worship) in Ambrose's exegesis and theology: G. FRANCESCONI, *Storia e simbolo. 'Mysterium in figura': la simbologia storico-sacramentale nel linguaggio e nella teologia di Ambrogio di Milano*, Brescia 1981; CH. JACOB, *'Arkandisziplin', Allegorese, Mystagogie. Ein neuer Zugang zur Theologie des Ambrosius von Mailand*, Frankfurt a. M. 1990 (Theophaneia, XXXII); B. STUDER, *Ambrogio di Milano teologo mistagogico*, in *Vescovi e pastori in epoca teodosiana*, Rome 1997, pp 569-586.

4

The Ambrosianum Mysterium Between Late Antiquity and The Early Middle Ages

Historical background

In 395 the emperor Theodosius died in Milan, and there too Ambrose died in 397. Only four years later Alaric and his Visigoths began their invasion of Italy; General Stilico had temporarily halted them at Pollentia, and again at Verona in 402. Milan no longer being considered safe, in that same year Theodosius' young son Honorius and his court left the city, settling in the port of Ravenna, defended by waters and marshes. The decision was a good one: at the end of 405 the Ostrogoths of Radagaisus spread as far as Tuscany, where Stilico had halted their progress at Fiesole in 406, with a victory attributed by local tradition to Ambrose's intercession.[1] The end of the same year saw the collapse of the Rhine defences and a stream of barbaric peoples spreading through the territories of the Prefecture of Gaul. Then in 410 came the traumatic sack of Rome by Alaric, taking prisoner Theodosius' daughter Galla Placidia.

In 476 the barbarian Odoacer deposed Romulus Augustulus, and installed himself in Ravenna as *Patricius Romanorum*; he was replaced in 493 by Theodoric, who had arrived in Italy at the head of his Ostrogoths. The institutions of the Empire were theoretically still in place, but in reality the political order and social makeup of the Roman west had been shattered by turbulent events. Especially in Italy, faced with dominant Germanic populations which although Christian were 'Arian' in faith ('non-Nicene' would be better), the 'Catholic' Church became the institution most representative of the 'Roman' section of the population in town and countryside. In the main Germanic centres beginning from Ravenna, alongside the buildings of the Church of the Romans where the *Legem Catholicam* was followed (i.e. the Nicene faith) and celebrations were in Latin, there were now places of worship of the Church of the Germans, marked by their own faith-tradition (the *Legem Gothorum*), a different discipline, and Gothic scriptures, translated by Ulfilas in the second half of the fourth century.

As already mentioned in the first chapter, the transfer of the western Imperial seat to Ravenna had its effects at the ecclesiastical level: from the beginning of the fifth century a vast metropolitical province formed around Aquileia, taking from Milan the sees of the eastern side of Italia Annonaria; and to the south of the Po the see of Ravenna, hierarchically subject to the Roman church, managed for the first time to gain the right of ordination of the neighbouring bishops of Flaminia and Picenum (those too being suburbicarian sees) and thereafter consolidated actual metropolitical power extending as far as Piacenza, the furthest north-western see of Aemilia, whose own episcopate at the time of Ambrose depended directly on the authority of the metropolitan of Milan.

1 PAULINUS. *Vita Ambrosii, L.2.*

Justinian's ascent to the throne in 527 and the launch of his military campaign to restore the Roman system in the west had tragic consequences for Milan. In 539 its faithfulness to the ideals of the empire, whose standards were welcomed triumphantly into the city, was repaid with devastation of the city and a terrible massacre of its inhabitants by the Gothic soldiers of Oraja when the city was briefly occupied again during the reign of Vitigis.

This political loyalty was soon combined with a no less firm religious opposition to imperial authority over the Edict of the Three Chapters with which Justinian between 543 and 545 sought to condemn the writing of Theodore of Mopsuestia and some statements of two other Antiochene fathers, Theodoret of Cyrus and Iba of Edessa, who at Chalcedon in 451 had been recognized as orthodox. The Milanese opposition was part of that of the whole west; and even though the metropolitan Datius, delayed by the Roman Pope Vigilius at Constantinople, was probably like him persuaded to accept the findings of the council of 553, dying straight afterwards on the shores of the Bosphorus, his church remained immoveable, together with the see of Aquileia, in what it saw as the defence of the Chalcedonian faith. Shortly after the middle of the sixth century in fact, the Roman Pope Pelagius relates that the bishops of the two northern metropolises ordained each other[1]: this practice of metropolitans ordaining metropolitans is a custom with many illustrious precedents and contemporary examples, and was ratified in Gaul in 538 in the third canon of the council of Orleans. Yet its appearance in Italy does not seem separable from the particular ecclesiastical situation which had come about there.

The deep doctrinal divide separating the churches of Milan and Aquileia from that of New Rome, but also from the Imperial see at Ravenna and the church of Rome, which by now had come into line, did not however harm the traditional faithfulness of the ecclesiastical hierarchies of the two Italian metropolises to the Empire as an ideal and an institution. The Lombard invasion shows this clearly.

Particularly in Milan, on the appearance of the new invaders in 569, the metropolitan Honoratus with the upper hierarchies of church and state abandoned the city, setting himself under the imperial standards in the port of Genoa, which with the Ligurian littoral remained Roman until the conquest by Rotari in 643 (or 642).

This period in imperial territory was not without consequences for the life of the Milanese church and for the entire metropolitical province. Already in the last decades of the sixth century Laurence II (occasionally called patriarch, following the usage in Gaul referred to in a letter of the Frankish king Childepert[2]) was constrained at Rome to condemn the Three Chapters, and underwent such pressure from Ravenna's archbishop as to insert his commemoration in the eucharistic diptychs.[3] No different was the fate in those few years of the bishop

---

1   *Epistula* LII.15.
2   MGH, *Epistolae*, III: *Epistolae Merovingici et Karolini Aevi*, I, p 151.
3   GREGORII I *Registrum*, IV: 2.37.

of Aquileia (for whom the title 'patriarch' had become standard usage from the mid-sixth century[1]): Severus, having taken refuge like his predecessor Elias in imperial territory on the lagoon-island of Grado, was led to Ravenna and forced to align himself with the condemnation of the Three Chapters and to declare his own communion with the local archbishop John.[2] In the case of Aquileia the reactions of bishops of the province led to Severus' retraction and, after his death, to the duplication of the patriarchate: the obsequious Condidianus having been nominated at Grado under the aegis of Ravenna, at Aquileia in 607 the bishops of the Lombard mainland elected John[3] (as is known, in 1451, in the province of Grado the title of patriarch passed to Venice, where in fact at that date already for some time the patriarch resided). As far as Milan was concerned, notwithstanding a similar attempt at a contrary election after the death of the Metropolitan Constans in 600, the institutional uniqueness of the province was safeguarded, but it was not possible to avoid internal tensions and divisions, still less the break-away of the see of Como, which from then on became part of the patriarchate of Aquileia, up until the suppression of the latter in 1751.

A direct reflection of these calamitous events of the end of the sixth century, and in particular of the decline with them of provincial solidarity, was the canonical and institutional weakening of the two bishops, of Aquileia in Grado and of Milan in Genoa. In effect, with the election at Genoa in 593 of the deacon Constans as successor to Laurence II, we see the Roman bishop intervening directly in the procedure for nominating the Milanese metropolitan, reserving to himself the assent to the elected candidate and confirming the election by sending the Petrine pallium (which probably was already given to Laurence after his adhesion to the condemnation of the Three Chapters).[4] Even heavier was the intervention in the institutional life of the see of Grado: after the flight of Patriarch Fortunatus who brought back to the mainland the treasures of the Aquileian church which had been transferred to Grado by Paulinus at the time of the Lombard invasion,[5] his successor Primigenius was directly nominated in 628 by the Roman Pope Honorius, who chose him from among his own subdeacons and sent him from Rome armed with the pallium and accompanied by precious gifts.[6]

The split between Aquileia and Rome and, for Milan, the tensions inside the province caused by the dispute over the Three Chapters, found definitive resolution in two synods held respectively in 680 (for the Milanese province, in preparation for the Council of Constantinople of 680/681 on monothelitism[7]) and (for the province of Aquileia) in 698 at Pavia.[8] The main architect of this

---

1 PELAGIUS I, Epistula XXIV; cf. .PAULUS Diaconus, Historia Langobardorum, III.25.
2 PAULUS Diaconus, Historia Langobardorum, III.26.
3 IOHANNES Aquileiensis, Epistula ad Agilulfum regem: MGH, Epistolae, III, p 639.
4 GREGORII I Registrum: III.29, 30, 31; XI.6, 14; IV.37.
5 PAULUS Diaconus, Historia Langobardorum, II.10.
6 Cronica de singulis patriarchis Nove Aquileie, ed. G. Monticolo, Cronache Veneziane Antichissime, I, Rome 1890, pp 10-11.
7 MANSI, XI cc. 203-208.
8 Carmen de synodo Ticinensi: MGH, Poetae Latini Aevi Carolini, IV.2-3, pp 728-731.

result was a Greek monk, Damian, who worked at the side of the metropolitan Mansuetus in 680 and who inspired the labours of the synod of 698, working on it directly as bishop of the Lombard royal city, Pavia.[1]

Besides resolving the Three-Chapters question in the Milanese province, the synod of 680 was extremely important too for another fundamental aspect of church life in the Lombard kingdom: the progressive integration of the Lombards themselves and their clergy into the church of the Romans. In the *sancta episcoporum fraternitas* which at that time surrounded the metropolitan Mansuetus, and whose members appear among the signatories to the *suggestio* of the Roman synod of 27 March 680, we find Anastasius as bishop of Pavia; he had been the 'Arian' bishop of the city and, on the death of the catholic bishop, had embraced the latter's faith, so inheriting his cathedra.[2] After little more than fifty years another Lombard, Theodorus, 'born of the royal line', became archbishop on the same metropolitan throne, and inheritor of the tradition of Ambrose, the consular Roman.

It is necessary to outline these profound ecclesiastical, institutional and social changes which marked the end of antiquity and beginning of the middle ages, for it is in this context that the Milanese church's inheritance was passed on and its future development, including that of the liturgy, was shaped.

At this time the clergy became structured into the two orders of cardinals and decumans characteristic of the whole medieval period. Presumably at this time the discipline of absolute continence for higher liturgical ministers, introduced by Ambrose and reaffirmed by the council of Turin of 398 (or 399) chaired by his successor Simplicianus, was replaced for priests and deacons by a discipline founded on ancient conciliar canons (marriage with a virgin, marriage before ordination, monogamy, ritual continence in relation to exercise of ministry). In the context of the changes in life and social rituals of those centuries, the custom of church blessing of marriages, attested by Ambrose, fell out of use, (even though obviously keeping the religious character of marriage, and consequently the bishop's responsibility for all discipline relating to it).

The sources, while scarce and patchy, do nevertheless show us the decisive importance of this period for the future course of Milanese church life and liturgy: they only document a few isolated instances of liturgical practice for us, however, and these can be better understood if placed in the context of earlier testimony from the time of Ambrose and of later documentation from the ninth century and onwards.

a. Continuity and evolution in initiation rites

This turbulent phase of the history was also the period in which Christianity, initially an urban phenomenon in Italy, began to spread in the countryside, the catholic church so becoming that of the 'Roman' population. The deacon Sisinnius, the reader Martyrius, and the hostiarius Alexander, martyred in Anaunia in May

---

1 PAULUS Diaconus, *Historia Langobardorum*, VI.4.
2 PAULUS Diaconus, *Historia Langobardorum*, IV.42.

397, give us a good example of the missionary activity launched by episcopal sees: but other evidence which can be gleaned from the preaching of Maximus of Turin and verified from archaeology (e.g. the small basilica of Garlate in Milanese ecclesiastical territory), point to the important role in this Christianization process of great families who had left the city to settle on land they owned in the countryside.

Away from the city Christian initiation rites inevitably saw the gradual disappearance of the imposition of hands (in Ambrose's time this, accompanied by the *invocatio* came after the anointing with chrism and the footwashing), which through its apostolic derivation (Acts 8.14-17) was exclusively episcopal. This rural development then influenced urban practice: a short mid-sixth-century mystagogical tract from Milan province makes no mention of the rite.[1] We find a like silence in the Ambrosian *Praeconium* which in evoking the Easter Vigil ceremonies strongly insists on chrismation and eucharist, and also in the hymn *Christe cunctorum* for Dedication Sunday, where the whole mysteric practice of the church is rehearsed: eucharistic celebration, baptismal laver, chrismation, penitence, anointing of the sick, deliverance of the possessed, commendation of the departed, consecration of church buildings. The absence of any episcopal hand-laying (or *consignatio*) in the Ambrosian liturgical books from then on is entirely consistent with the evidence from late antiquity.

Sources from a Gallican milieu enable us to trace the evolution. At the end of the fourth century, canon 77 of the collection entitled 'of Elvira' sets the principle that for the baptism rite performed by priests or deacons without a bishop, i.e.in rural situations, the bishop *'per benedictionem perficere debebit'* (must complete it by the blessing); then in 441, canon 2 of Orange provides that episcopal confirmation take the form of a simple blessing (as in the Milan of Ambrose), excluding the practice, evidently well known, but alien in the sense of being exclusively Roman, of a second chrismation; still in the fifth century, in Homily XXIX [XXVIII] of so-called Eusebius Gallicanus we find a solemn episcopal confirmation on Pentecost Sunday; finally, in the sacramentaries of the seventh and eighth centuries (*Gothicum, Bobiense, Gallicanum Vetus*) there is a total absence of any reference to an episcopal confirmation rite, and the order for initiation (not mentioning other elements such as the vesting and the 'crown') is as in the Ambrosian books: baptismal lavacrum, chrismation, footwashing.

Joseph Levesque, analysing the formularies in the Gallican books, has shown how on a christological and pneumatological basis these books concentrate in the chrismation after the baptismal bath the meanings and mysterical contents attributed by the preceding Latin patristic tradition to episcopal confirmation: 'the rites celebrated were adequate and complete as a celebration of full Christian Initiation'. It is therefore not by chance that in Milan between the eleventh and twelfth centuries Landulfus (so-called) applied the expression *'baptizatus et confirmatus'* to the Ambrosian initiation ceremony in which, after the baptismal

---

1   PL, LVII, cc. 771-782.

bath, the chrismation and footwashing, no *confirmatio* by the archbishop is envisaged.[1]

It is worth noting that this development in initiation practice and its exegesis was not limited to the Gallican and Milanese areas; the attribution of the content of the ancient invocation for the *Spiritale signaculum* (exclusively episcopal rite) to the post-baptismal chrismation (not reserved to the bishop) had an illustrious precedent in the east: practice at Jerusalem as reported in the fourth-fifth century by the mystagogical catecheses of John is something we still see today in the initiation rites of the churches of Constantinopolitan tradition.

b. Dedication of churches and ordination of bishops

Ambrosian sacramental actions strictly reserved to the bishop in some cases lack any ritual documentation, since from the Carolingian period, and at all events from the tenth century, the pontificals used by the Milanese archbishops were books belonging to the Romano-Frankish tradition. Very important here is the small fascicule dated to the eleventh century inserted at the end of the contemporary codex 605 (*olim* LXXXIIII) of the Capitular Library of Lucca: it describes with somewhat formal fastidiousness the Ambrosian *ordo* for consecration of churches and altars, followed by prayers at the blessing of fonts together with the actual blessing of the same, blessing of chrism with corresponding preface, and blessing of oil. Most of this material has also been transmitted by Milanese liturgical books in the rites for Holy Saturday and Maundy Thursday (especially the Missals and Manuals), but the Ambrosian *ordo* for dedication of churches comes to us only via this unique source; not only does it testify to these early medieval elements of the Ambrosian liturgy lost through Carolingian interference, or disappearing in its wake: it also gives unequivocal evidence of specific Ambrosian formularies, perhaps fixed on scrolls, for the solemn ritual acts of the episcopal and metropolitical ministry of the archbishop. The *ordo* combines in its own way the different ritual elements typical of the dedication of churches in the west, and not only that.

In front of the locked doors of the church, after the greeting, the archbishop proceeds to asperge the outside walls, beginning with the right hand side (that is, moving in an anticlockwise direction). Back at the royal doors, he traces a cross with his pastoral staff and writes the alphabet on the walls (an Irish origin has been suggested for this, but it has also been related to the *Chrismon S. Ambrosii* with Alpha and Omega incised in marble and fixed to the internal apse wall of the cathedral, and also to the pre-baptismal catechesis on Chrismon, Alpha and Omega, traced with ash *super cilicium in medio ecclesiae*, a catechesis described by 'Landulfus'[2]).

Straight after there is anointing with chrism in the form of a cross repeated

1   L(ANDULFUS). *Historia Mediolanensis*, I.9.
2   L(ANDULFUS). *Historia Mediolanensis*, I.12.

three times on each side of the building, immediately followed by attachment to the walls themselves of three *'candelas'* for each side. The triple dialogue beween the archbishop (striking the door with his staff) and a deacon (the only person inside the church) precedes the opening of the royal doors:

'Tollite portas principes (-pis) vestri et introibit rex gloriae' / 'Quis est iste rex gloriae?' / a) 'Dominus fortis et potens'; b) 'Dominus potens in prelio'; c) 'Dominus virtutum, ipse est rex gloriae'.

After this third response the archbishop opens with his staff the royal doors and all enter the church to the singing of the antiphon *Intrate portas eius in confessione.* Aspersion with water follows, then the writing of the alphabet in the ashes spread in the form of a cross on the floor, the three crosses traced with chrism on each wall and the fixing of the respective twelve candles. At the end of this the archbishop goes out of the church and stands in front of its doors, gives a greeting and says a prayer. He then goes into the church and at its centre recites a new prayer; two formulas are provided: the first (present with variations also in the Gellone Sacramentary) refers to the 'house of prayer' which God has desired to be consecrated to him and arranged as a worthy setting for the celebration of the divine mysteries (*Omn. semp. Deus, qui sacrari tibi locum orationis domus usibusque mysterii tui aptari voluisti*); the second (present also in the Sacramentary 'Vat. Reg. Lat. 316', the so-called Gelasian) refers to a place of worship 'purified from the deep darkness of heresy', asking that those who worship there may 'persevere steadfast in the unity of the holy Trinity and in the Catholic faith'.

There is possibly an echo here of that process - developed at the tail-end of late antiquity and referred to above - through which in Italy too the Germanic 'Arian' element became completely integrated into the institutions and religious traditions of the local churches of the Romans.

Once the building has been dedicated, there comes the dedication of the altar. After the archbishop's greeting and the washing of the altar to the singing of psalm LXXXIII (LXXXIV), there follows a brief invocation formula and a longer dedicatory prayer (this too having parallels in ancient western pontificals).

There is no mention of the translation of the relics followed by a eucharistic celebration. We can rightly suppose that these elements connected with the dedication rite were the subject of a further specific *ordo*, as the *Ordines Romani* XLII and XLIII of Andrieu suggest, and as happens among the Greeks.

Besides the *ordo* for the dedication of churches the manuscript sources have preserved odd traces, quite tenuous to be sure, of an Ambrosian ritual for the ordination of bishops. In the Lodrino Manual (Milan, Bibl. Amb., MS. A 246 Suss., f. 64 v.) there is in effect a form for ordination of bishops, with divine office, mass, triple *psallentium* (procession chant), and with the acclamations of the clergy and people for the one elected. The term 'Papa' ('Pope') used in the latter (*Dignus es, iustus es, ill., papa tu eris*) goes back without doubt to a late antique/early medieval phase when in the Latin west this term was also used in reference to bishops, as the curious Latin epigraph in Greek letters dated to the eighth or

43

ninth centuries confirms for the Milanese milieu: here Ambrose is described as *ΠΑΠΑ ΑΙΚΛΑΙ ΜΑΙΔΗΛΑΝΕΝCHC: papa aecl(esi)ae Maedi[o]llanensis.*[1]

c. The Morning Office and its Irish connections

No written evidence of the daily offices survives from pre-Carolingian times. Traces of it can be found, however, in sources outside the Milanese church which were influenced by it.

First of all there is in the Spanish *Liber Orationum Psalmographus,* an archaic collection of Ambrosian psalm-collects identified by Jordi Pinell, of which no trace remains in the Milanese ecclesial office, but might perhaps have been used in the *Vigiliae,* when the whole psalter was sung.

More eloquent is the testimony to the structure of the morning office in the Irish Antiphoner of Bangor of 680-691. Besides the final doxology of the *Laus Angelorum Magna* (*Gloria et honor Deo Patri*), there is in this insular monastic collection a celebrative structure of Lauds taking the form of a fixed succession of canticles and psalms with their own collects analogous to that of the Ambrosian Sunday office attested to in post-Carolingian Milanese sources: *Benedictio S. Zachariae* (Benedictus), *Canticum Moysi* (Cantemus Domino), *Benedictio trium puerorum* (Benedicite), Laudate psalms.

d. The eucharist

Different parts of the St Gall codex, Stiftsbibliothek, 908, and also the ff. 16 v and 19 v of the Zurich codex, Zentralbibliothek, C 79b, represent—as has been well shown by the editor Alban Dold—the re-use of pages originally bearing written Ambrosian liturgical texts.

Pages 157-158, 161-164, 167-168 of the St Gall codex come from an Ambrosian liturgical manuscript of the seventh century. Interest in these documents has encouraged Patrizia Carmassi to carry out a new and careful analysis of them. In reference to these pages she correctly speaks, not of a sacramentary, but of a *libellus missarum.* In effect certain texts are penned here which seem to have been for the celebrations of the eucharist on Sundays (and ferias) which did not already have their own formularies. We find the Gloria in excelsis Deo followed by the *Quiriaeleison,* then four Gospel pericopes (present in pre-Carolingian times on the Sundays after Pentecost) and four prayers.

If this archaic testimony allows us definitely to say that already in the seventh century in the Milanese church the singing of the Gloria on Sundays was established (concluded—as with other ritual elements—with a triple Kyrie in Ambrosian milieux), as regards the overall structure of the celebration further insights can be drawn from the the the analysis of the later St.Simplicianus Missal (Milan, Bibl. Cap. Metrop., ms. II.D.3.3, dated between the last quarter of the ninth century and the beginning of the tenth).

---

1 U. MONNERET DE VILLARD. *Catalogo delle Iscrizioni cristiane anteriori al secolo XI,* Milan 1915. N° 13.

Above all in this codex, which is interesting in various ways and to which we shall return, after the *'Pacem habete'* and before the *oratio super sindonem* which precedes the offertory, there is the invitation to the faithful, *'Corrigite vos ad orationem'*. This invitation, besides explaining the response *'Ad Te, Domine'* (which, in referring directly to the *'Pacem habete'* in the most common form of the *ordo missae*, had become absolutely enigmatic) and besides explaining the *'Pacem habete'* as a formal announcement of the exchange of peace (which happened therefore before the offertory rites), clearly shows the positioning of the diaconal litany, followed by the kneeling faithful, in the Ambrosian eucharist in the pre-Carolingian period. The latter re-connects Milan to the most general and ancient tradition of the churches and also shows clear parallels with Gallican practice.

But also the euchology of the *Missal of St Simplicianus*, analysed in an exemplary manner by Judith Frei, yields further very interesting data. Placing this euchology in comparison with that of the surviving Ambrosian sacramentaries and, more in general, with western euchological texts, the German abbess has identified especially for the fifth week of Lent an archaic Ambrosian redaction of eucharistic texts for the ferias of that special period of the year. Besides confirming the a-liturgical practice on Fridays in Lent, and the daily celebration of the eucharist on the other ferias (as Ambrose already attests and was also practised in Gaul), such formularies suggest a structure which lacked a variable post-communion prayer (as in the Bobbio Missal, a manuscript of Gallican origin, which in its formularies does not go beyond the *Contestatio* ('preface'), and which in the daily *Missa Romensis* manifests the use of a fixed Canon of Roman type with post-communion and *consummatio missae*). Consequently, in the phase preceding the Carolingian reorganization, the celebration would seem to have included, after the preface (a typically variable element in Ambrosian practice), a fixed sequence of elements of which the eucharistic prayer itself was a part.

Here we encounter the problem of the text of the eucharistic prayer in use at Milan in late antiquity. This question is made particularly complex by the extracts, varying in fullness, of Gallican eucharistic prayers preserved in the forms for Thursday and Saturday of Holy Week in the Carolingian books. Morin in his time proposed that these texts be seen as relics of eucharistic prayers in use in Milan before the adoption of the Roman Canon. This fascinating hypothesis cannot affect the sixth-seventh-century dating suggested by Coebergh for these Gallican fragments, on which the influence of the sacramentaries of Roman form, especially those of Gelasian type, is already identifiable. In addition, the form given in the codices of the Carolingian period shows the insertion of these Gallican formularies into Roman-type structural elements of the Canon. It is not possible to identify clearly when this contamination came about, and whether it is to be understood as reception of Gallican texts into the euchological scheme of the Canon or vice versa, and whether in the Ambrosian milieu the text in the form which has come down to us is 'original', or the result of a later revision. In fact our information on

45

liturgical euchology and on its written fixing in the disturbed centuries before the Carolingian period are too fragmentary (and not only in the Ambrosian milieu) to be able to trace a complete picture. It is certain anyway that in that period Milan both gave and received, as is attested by the Hispanic eucharistic formularies for the Sundays of Lent, which could be called a euchological development of the Ambrosian prefaces.

With regard to ceremonial aspects of the eucharist, one in particular, related to the readings, is positively attested from the sixth century: no minister was (or is) allowed to begin to read sacred scripture without the presiding bishop giving a mandate by means of a blessing. Gregory of Tours speaks of this as an Ambrosian custom in the De virtutibus sancti Martini episcopi[1], in a well-known passage which in Carolingian times was taken up at Milan in the De vita et meritis Ambrosii[2], and given a permanent visual embodiment on the golden altar of Vuolvinius[3] in the basilica of St Ambrose and in the mosaic of the half-dome of the apse.[4]

With reference to the ff. 77, 83, 116 of the palimpsest codex 908 of St Gall and to the ff. 16 and 19 of the Zurich MS. C79b, the editor has claimed to be able to attribute them to a Liber antiphonarius ecclesiae Mediolanensis written shortly after the seventh century; they contain some chants for the eucharist, especially those for Easter Day. Such manuscripts indicate the order of chants in the celebration and their classification, both confirmed by later evidence; in certain cases the particular Ambrosian nomenclature is also given: Ingressa Confractorium.

The Ambrosian musical tradition therefore seems to have known a stabilization which was earlier and above all independent of the complex development of the euchology. It is no accident therefore to find that a prose poem in praise of Milan and its metropolitical see, the Versum de Mediolano civitate, edited in an ecclesiastical milieu in the time of King Liutprand and archbishop Theodore (roughly 732 - 744), expressly describes people's admiration for the melodies and chants of this church.

e. Lections in the Ambrosian tradition

Debates on the origin of the Milanese liturgical tradition have mostly focussed on the euchological inheritance, seeking to identify its stages of redaction and its borrowings from other traditions, especially those of Roman type. There has been talk of a mid-fifth-century redaction, and of a further one in the seventh

---

1   GREGORIUS Touronensis, De virtutibus sancti Martini episcopi, I.5: MGH, Script. Rer. Merov., I.2, p 591.
2   De vita et meritis Ambrosii, 79.
3   cf. C.CAPPONI (ed.), L'Altare d'Oro di Sant'Ambrogio, Banca Agricola Milanese, 1996.
4   C. BERTELLI: Mosaici a Milano, in Atti del 10° Congresso internazionale di Studi sull'Alto Medioevo: Milano e i Milanesi prima del Mille. Milan 1983, Spoleto 1986, pp 331-341; Opere d'arte per la chiesa Ambrosiana. Il mosaico alla luce della tradizione apostolica milanese, in: Il mosaico di Sant'Ambrogio: Storia del mosaico e dei suoi restauri, ed. C. CAPPONI, Genoa 1997, pp 6-18; Mosaici a Milano dall'età paleocristiana ai carolingi, in: La pittura a Milano, ed. M. Gregori, .

century (during the period torn apart by the crisis of the Three Chapters), before the systematic work carried out in the Carolingian period which initially would have come about—according to Frei—in a number of separate stages.

In reality the tradition of a church, and of the Milanese in particular, seems in the late antique and early medieval centuries to be tied not so much to individual texts of prayers (in those times anyway still at the stage of evolution) as to ecclesial catechesis. This came into its own in the rites of initiation and was connected to a precise system of scripture readings which characterized not only initiation but all the most important solemnities and feasts of the year.

The liturgical systematization of the biblical pericopes has a special importance for the unique identity of the Milanese church, something quite clear in the period of the Lombards, as the prose poem in praise of the city and its church attests, above all mentioning the rich ordering of the lessons, solidly structured (*pollens ordo lectionum*). So-called Landulfus could be echoing this text in the eleventh-twelfth century, pointing in his apologia for the Milanese church to this expression in the lectionary of the '*Ambrosianum Mysterium*', on which—he says—Gregory the Great himself had drawn in editing the liturgical books of the church of Rome.[1]

Already in Ambrose's sermons and more generally in his writings it has been possible to sift out the elements of an annual cycle of celebrations, with Easter as the central pillar, but also containing a feast of the manifestation of the divine Word in the flesh, and a certain number of anniversaries of saints. We have seen that certain days were marked by the reading of set lesssons, as in the Paschal Triduum, Great Week and Easter week, readings which were seen by Ambrose as '*de more*' (customary). Lent as well, by now fully developed, had a catechetical cycle stabilized in general outline at least.

In the following period this ancient nucleus not only became a settled system, but round about it—and in a way modelled on it—the entire yearly cycle was reaching definition.

At Milan also the manifestation of the Word in the flesh had already for some time been taking shape as a double celebration on 25 December and 6 January (the hymn *Illuminans Altissime*, however, comes from after Ambrose's time).[2] Next, on the model of Easter, the need was felt to prepare for the solemn annual commemoration of the Incarnation by prefixing it with a time for more intense prayer and recollection: a cycle of six weeks, starting with the Sunday after 11 November, and coming to be known as the *Lent of St Martin*.[3]

---

1   '*Quasi bonam olivam atque fructiferam in oleastro inseruit*': L(andulfus). *Historia Mediolanensis, II.6.*
2   AMBROISE de Milan. *Hymnes.* Texte établi, traduit et annoté sous la direction de J. FONTAINE. Paris 1992
3   Cf. the false *Praeceptum* of the Lombard king Astolfus dated 18 February 753, edited about the middle of the ninth century on the basis of earlier material: ed. C. BRÜHL. *Codice Diplomatico Longobardo*, III.1. Rome 1973 (Istituto Storico Italiano per il Medio Evo. Fonti per la Storia d'Italia, LXIV), p 164; as well as the later false *Praeceptum* of Desiderius dated 16 February 759: *Ibid*, p.201, 1.25.

An extension of the period of preparation for Easter, meanwhile, was taken over from fourth-century Jerusalem where it is already attested at this period, and was spreading throughout the east: as in Holy Week this development of the rites left no more space for the catechesis of the *competentes*, another week was added to Jerusalem's six (*Quinquagesima*), in order not to disturb the continuity of their instruction, and under monastic influence another octave was added (*Sexagesima*) in order to complete, after the model of Christ in the wilderness, the 40 days of fasting (it needs to be remembered here that in Milan, as in eastern practice, it was forbidden to fast not only on Sundays but also on Saturdays).

Besides that, in the Easter season the feast of the Ascension took shape (naturally without a vigil), and with it was associated the triduum of the *Letaniae*.

The season after Pentecost appears too in the pre-Carolingian *Evangelistary of Busto* as already systematized, with the two capstones of the *Decollatio sancti Iohannis* (Beheading of John the Baptist, 29 August; the following Sunday is called *Dominica post Decollatione*) and the *Dedication of the church* (Third Sunday in October, preceded by the *Dominica ante Transmigratione*, that is, Sunday before the transferral from the 'summer' church to the 'winter' church on the day of the Dedication festival). It is significant, however, that the readings for this period (as in fact those for ferias of Lent) do not appear in the *Capitulary*, and that in the *Evangelistary* they make up a separate block described as '*de cottidianis diebus*' (for ordinary days), developing basically as semi-continuous reading from Matthew, Mark and Luke in succession. All in all this may reflect a more archaic phase, when the Sundays after Pentecost had not yet acquired a particular identity, even though a set order of lessons had already been established for them. This is implied also by the seventh-century *libellus missarum* in the St Gall palimpsest 908, where beside 'common' prayer forms there are four gospel pericopes: three from Matthew about miracles of Christ (Mt 8.23-26; 15.21-28; 9.1-8; the first and the third are also present in the Busto codex), followed by Jn 8.3-11 (the woman taken in adultery: a pericope commented on by Ambrose in an ecclesiological sense, and set for the Sunday before the Dedication). Not dissimilar is the testimony of the sixth/seventh-century pages on which an impression survives in MS 184 (161) of the Orleans Municipal Library and in which are indicated the following passages: Mt. 8.28-9.8 (cf, in the *Busto Evangelistary;* Mt. 8.28-34 and 9.1-8); 2 Cor. 9.10-15; Mt. 9.18-23 (cf. *Busto Evangelistary;* Mt. 9.18-26).

The period after Epiphany does not yet appear as fully developed in the Busto codex, which provides only two set readings in the Capitulary, rising to four in the Evangelistary.

Patrizia Carmassi, already mentioned more than once, has devoted her far-reaching research to reconstructing the various phases of development of this cycle of readings. On the basis of extensive documentation of codices stretching from late antique *tetraevangelia* (the *codex Vercellensis*, with pre-Jerome text, is dated to the fourth century) and from their marginal annotations from the sixth to the eighth centuries, right up to the late medieval sources, she has been able to document an unbroken continuity in the use of some texts which were already present in the time of Ambrose. In addition there is agreement among definitely Milanese sources on many points, as also in sources relating to other churches, whether in the ancient ecclesiastical province or (referring to a few specific aspects) the rest of Italy and Gaul.

The reading of Genesis and Proverbs on the ferias of Lent, mentioned in *De mysteriis* and documented once again at Milan from the ninth century, has—for example—for the pre-Carolingian phase an unusual attestation in a manuscript, once again Irish, from the eighth century: the fragment H.Omont No.1 of the Catholic University Library of Louvain.

Beyond odd pieces of provision in Christmastide and Eastertide the cycle in the Busto manuscript—from the first Sunday of Advent to Pentecost—was substantially confirmed by the Carolingian revisers; to them on the other hand is due the completion of the texts for the period after Epiphany and the new and well-defined provision of pericopes for the Sundays after Pentecost and after the Beheading of John Baptist.

The readings for feasts and the periods making up the annual cycle (but also the major saints' celebrations, as is suggested by the presence of the *Depositio* of St Ambrose in the St Gall palimpsest already cited, No. 908, f.111) were, then, already established and fixed in Ambrosian usage in the pre-Carolingian period: in the first part of the eighth century we can confidently speak of *pollens ordo lectionum*. Here we have an organic lection system which in various of its elements, passed on in subsequent ages, shows a precious continuity with practice as known in the time of Ambrose, and is in significant agreement with other ecclesiastical areas of the Latin west. In this way, on the eve of the Frankish conquest of Italy it is possible to see in the liturgical practice of the Milanese church, besides both continuity and developments in its tradition, the reflection too of the communion of the churches which was coming to exist in the later patristic centuries, with their institutional ordering and their flexible ways of bringing it to realization. In this sense, what we can discover of forms of worship in the Milanese church and those churches which in antiquity it influenced in various ways only confirms the novelty of Carolingian ecclesiastical policy and the decisive significance that had for the formation of the historic identity of the Christian west and its institutional and ecclesiological evolution.

Bibliographical note

For an **outline of Milanese history** in the centuries after Ambrose see volume II of *Storia di Milano*, Fondazione Treccani degli Alfieri, Milan 1954; cf. also *Il millennio ambrosiano*, I: *Milano, una capitale da Ambrogio ai Carolingi*, cur. C. BERTELLI, Milan 1987; on the specifically ecclesiastical and religious aspects: *Diocesi di Milano*, I, ed.. A. CAPRIOLI, A. RIMOLDI, L. VACCARO, Brescia-Gazzada 1990 (Storia religiosa della Lombardia, IX).

On the pair: *legem Gothorum / legem catholicam*, with reference to the religious origins of the term *lex* already present in the *Edict of Thessalonica* (27.2.380: *Codex Theodosianus*, XVI, 1, 2, ed. TH. MOMMSEN, I, 2, Berolini 1905, p 833. 7-9): G. MARINI, *I papiri diplomatici*, Rome 1805, N° CXIX, pp 181-182; AGNELLI *Liber Pontificalis Ecclesiae Ravennatis*: De sancto Victore, ed. A. TESTI RASPONI, Bologna 1924 (RR II SS, nova ed., II, 3), p 188. 19. On the Lombard period, full documentation can be found in: *Longobardi e Lombardia: aspetti di civiltà longobarda. Atti del VI Congresso Internazionale di Studi sull' Alto Medievo. Milano, 21-25 ottobre 1978*, Spoleto 1980. On Milan during the Three Chapters crisis see C. ALZATI, *'Pro sancta fide, pro dogma patrum'. La tradizione dogmatica delle Chiese italiche di fronte alla questione dei Tre Capitoli. Caratteri dottrinali e implicazioni ecclesiologiche dello scisma*, in *Como e Aquileia. Per una storia della società comasca (612-1751). Atti del Convegno. Como, 15-17 ottobre 1987*, Como 1991 (Società Storica Comense. Raccolta Storica, XIX), pp 49-82 (aa also in *Ambrosiana Ecclesia* [cit.], pp 97-130). On the tricapitoline crisis in the ecclesiastical province of Aquileia and the duplication of the patriarchal see: G. CUSCITO, *Fede e politica ad Aquileia. Dibattito teologico e centri di potere (secoli IV-VI)*, Udine 1987 (Università degli Studi di Trieste. Facoltà di Magistero. III Serie, XIX).

On the liturgy of Aquileia Baumstark Baumstark also wrote at the beginning of this century, in a monograph which, while dated, is as always stimulating (A. BAUMSTARK, *Liturgia romana e liturgia dell'Esarcato: Il rito detto in seguito patriarchino e le origini del Canon missae romano*, Roma 1904); a little later, in the wake of G. MORIN, *L'année liturgique à Aquilée anterieurement à l'époque carolingienne*, 'Revue Bénédictine', XIX (1902), pp 1-12, there came the work of G. VALE – P. PASCHINI, *Gli antichi usi liturgici nella Chiesa di Aquileia dalla Domenica delle Palme alla Domenica di Pasqua*, Padova 1907. A decisive contribution to our knowledge of ancient liturgical practice in Aquileia, in many ways related to that of Milan, has come in the studies on the Homiliary of bishop Chromatius († 407/408) by J. LEMARIÉ (see in particular his publications in: CROMACE d'Aquilée, *Sermons*, Paris 1969 [SCh, CLIV], pp 82-108; *Aquileia e Milano*, Aquileia 1973 [Antichità Altoadriatiche, IV], pp 249-170; *Aquileia e Ravenna*, Aquileia 1978 [Antichità Altoadriatiche, VIII], pp 355-373). Cf. also M. HULGO, *Liturgia e musica sacra aquileiese*, in *storia della cultura veneta I* (Vincenza, 1976) pp 312-??? On medieval sources the recent writings of G. PERESSOTTI: *Il Messale Aquileiese secondo alcuni codici del Medioevo*, 'Ephemerides Liturgicae', CXI (1997), pp 448-475; *Sequenze e letture evangeliche nel Messale Aquileiese*, 'Ephemerides Liturgicae', CXII (1998), pp 127-148. Particularly on the 'patriarchine rite' used by the church of Como from the time of its transferred allegiance to the patriarchate of Aquileia: A. CODAGHENGO, *Il rito patriarchino e consuetudini della Chiesa d'Aquileia già in vigore nella Diocesi di Como sino alla fine del secolo XVI*, 'Memorie Storiche Forogiuliesi', XLIV (1960-1961), pp 25-51; S. CELLA, *Il rito patriarchino di Como*, in *Ricerche Storiche sulla Chiesa Ambrosiana*, I, Milan 1970, (Archivio Ambrosiano, XVIII), pp 44-82; C. MARCORA, *Il rito patriarchino*, in *Como e Aquileia* (cit.), Como 1991, pp 123-139. This patriarchine consciousness was also present in the episcopal territory of Milan, at Monza and its dependencies, something still referred to at the time of Charles Borromeo (I. SCHUSTER, *Lo scisma dei Tre Capitoli ed il Rito Patriarchino a Monza*, 'La Scuola Cattolica', LXXI [1943], pp 81-94; T. ABBIATI, *Il Rito Ambrosiano a Monza secondo una corrispondenza inedita di San Carlo*, 'La Scuola Cattolica', LXVIII [1940], pp 201 ff.). In reality this 'patriarchine' identity was already in medieval times—above all in areas on the periphery—more of an 'ecclesiological consciousness' than a real inheritance of texts and usages of Aquileian origin, given the Romanization which from the Carolingian period developed in Aquileia itself. On this, based on liturgical manuscripts from Monza (cf. M. FERRARI – G. BELLONI, with additions by L. TOMEI, *La Biblioteca Capitolare di Monza*, Padova 1974 [Medioevo e Umanesimo, XXI]), B. G. BAROFFIO has spoken of an 'island of the Roman rite': *La Biblioteca Capitolare*, in *Il Duomo di Monza*, II: *I Tesori*, cur. R. CONTI, Milan 1989, p 183. Similar opinions are expressed by T. DELL'ORO, in reference to the *Liber Ordinarius Modoetiensis* of the first half of the 13th century (cf. R. MAMBRETTI, *Il contributo dell'Obituario e del "Liber ordinarius" della chiesa monzese alla storia edilizia del Duomo*, in *Monza anno 1300. La basilica di S: Giovanni Battista e la sua facciata*, ed. R. CASSANELLI, Monza 1988, pp 136-141), in the edition of this text in the *Monumenta Italiae Liturgica*, volume II. A liturgical tradition is not in fact reducible to either text or ceremonial—it is above all an awareness of ecclesial consciousness capable of carrying itself forward by the strength of its own solidity, and so able to transform elements from other traditions which it takes into itself.

On Ambrosian connections with Hispanic liturgy, with specific reference to psalm-collects: J. PINELL, *Liber Orationum Psalmographus. Colectas de salmos del antiguo rito hispánico. Recomposición y edición crítica*, Barcelona-Madrid 1972 (Monumenta Hispaniae Sacra. S. Liturgica, IX). Parallels with the Milanese ecclesial morning office in the *Antiphonary of Bangor* (in which the *transitus*, '*corpus christi accepimus*', also appears) have been closely analysed by M. CURRAN, *The Antiphonary of Bangor and the Early Irish Monastic Liturgy*, Dublin 1984.

Witnesses to **the pre-Carolingian Ambrosian liturgical inheritance** preserved in the St Gall codex, Stiftsbibliothek, *908*, and the Zurich codex, Zentralbibliothek, C *79bV*, have been edited by A. DOLD: *Le text de la Missa catechumenorum du Cod. Sang. 908*, 'Revue Bénédictine', XXXVI (1924), pp 307-316; *Getligte Paulus- und Psalmentexte unter getligten ambrosianischen Liturgiestücken aus Codex Sangallensis 908*, Beuron 1928 (Texte und Arbeiten, XIV); '*Enthenticus-authenticus*'. *Ein Termin im St. Galler Palimpsest 908 und seine Stellung in der Liturgiegeschichte*, 'Münchener theologische Zeitschrift', XI (1960), pp 262-266; *Dove si trovano le più antiche tracce della Messa milanese*, 'Quaderni di Ambrosius' [Supplemento ad 'Ambrosius', XXXVII (1961)], pp 3-15. On the sixth/seventh-century codex impression surviving in MS 184 (161) of the Orleans Municipal Library; K. GAMBER, *Leimbdrücke eines mailändischen Lektionars aus dem 6./7. Jahrhundert*, 'Scriptorium', XV (1961), pp 117-121.

In particular on the diaconal *preces* which followed the dismissal of the catechumens: P. DE CLERCK, *La 'prière universelle' dans les liturgies anciennes. Témoinages patristiques et textes liturgiques*, Münster Westfalen 1977 (Liturgiewissenschaftliche Quellen und Forschungen, LXII). For a similar original location of this in Greek usage: A. STRITMATTER: *Notes on the Byzantine Synapte*, 'Traditio', X (1954), pp 51-108; *A Peculiarity of the Slavic Liturgy found in Greek Euchologies*, in *Late Classical and Medieval Studies in Honour of Albert Mathias Friend Jr.*, ed. K. WEITZMANN, Princeton University Press, 1955, pp 197-203; on its later transferral to the beginning of the service, witnessed at the end of the ninth century: J. MATEOS, *La célébration de la parole dans la liturgie byzantine*, Rome 1971 (OCA, 191), pp 29-31. On the ancient connection between kiss of peace and prayers of the faithful, later abandoned in Greek usage: R. TAFT, *The Great Entrance*, Rome 1975 (OCA, 200), pp 50-51, 375-378.

On **prayers of the eucharist on ferias in Lent**, identified by J. FREI, see the *Einleitung* to the edition of *Messale di San Simpliciano* edited by her: *Das ambrosianische Sakramentar D 3-3 aus dem mailändischen Metropolitankapitel* (cit.), Münster 1974, pp 42 ff. On the various problems connected with the Ambrosian eucharistic prayers of Maundy Thursday and Holy Saturday, it is sufficient here to indicate the various positions in the debate: P. CAGIN, *Les archaïsmes combinés des deux canons ambrosiens du Jeudi Saint et de la nuit de Pâques*, in *L'Eucharistie. Canon primitif de la Messe*, Paris 1912, pp 91 ff.; L. DUCHESNE, *Origines du culte chrétien*, Paris 1925⁵, p 227; G. MORIN: *L'origine del canone ambrosiano a proposito di particolarità gallicane nel giovedì e sabato santo*, 'Ambrosius', III (1927), pp 75-77; *Depuis quand un Canon fixe à Milan? Restes de ce qu'il a remplacé*, 'Revue Bénédictine', LI (1939), pp 101-108 (It.transl.: 'Ambrosius', XVII [1941], pp 89-93); C. COEBERGH, *Tre antiche anafore della liturgia di Milano*, 'Ambrosius', XXIX (1953), pp 219-232; FREI, *Einleitung* (cit.), pp 149-153.

Attempts to identify **the pre-Carolingian redactional stages of the Ambrosian sacramentary** (perhaps it is more prudent to speak of euchological heritage) have been undertaken by A. PAREDI, *I prefazi ambrosiani. Contributo alla storia della Liturgia latina*, Milan 1937 (a first redaction from the mid-5th century), by O. HEIMING, *Aliturgische Fastenferien in Mailand*, 'Archiv für Liturgiewissenschaft', II (1952), pp 44-66 (7th century, in the context of the Genoan exile, and under influence of Ravenna; a possible mediation by Ravenna has also been suggested for the oriental elements which came into the Ambrosian musical repertory: M. HUGLO, *Antifone antiche per la Fractio Panis*, 'Ambrosius', XXXI [1955], pp 85-95), and also by A. M. TRIACCA, *Per una migliore ambientazione delle fonti liturgiche ambrosiane sinassico-eucaristiche. Note metodologiche*, in *Fons vivus. Miscellanea liturgica Dom Vismara*, Zürich 1971, pp 205-215 (second redaction in the context of the Lombard renaissance).

The **readings-cycle in pre-Carolingian times** has an authoritative witness in the Capitulary and Evangelistary of Busto Arsizio: P. BORELLA, *Il Capitolare ed Evangeliario di S. Giovanni Battista in Busto Arsizio*, 'Ambrosius', X (1934), pp 210-232; A. PAREDI, *L'Evangeliario di Busto Arsizio*, in *Miscellanea liturgica Card. Giacomo Lercaro*, II, Rome-Paris-Tournai-New York 1967, pp 207-249. For a study of the testimonies relating to the 'Italian' area, that is the ancient Italia Annonaria, see the study by P. CARMASSI cited in the Bibliographical note to chapter II.

On the **evolution of Christian initiation practice** in the late antique centuries see C. ALZATI, '*Baptizatus et confirmatus*'. *Considerazioni sull'iniziazione cristiana a Milano tra tarda antichità e medioevo*, in *Studi in onore di Mons. Angelo Majo per il suo 70° compleanno*, ed. F. RUGGERI, Milan 1996 (Archivio Ambrosiano, LXXIII), pp 23-37. On the demoting of church blessing for conjugal pact: E. CATTANEO, *La celebrazione delle noze a Milano*, in *Ricerche Storiche sulla Chiesa Ambrosiana*, VI, Milan 1976 (Archivio Ambrosiano, XXIX), pp 144 ff. [also. in *La Chiesa di Ambrogio* (cit.), Milan 1984, pp 270 ff.]. Regarding the *Ordo Ambrosianus ad consecrandam aecclesiam et altaria*, preserved in cod. *605* of the Chapter Library of Lucca, see the edition edited by G. MERCATI, in *Antiche reliquie liturgiche ambrosiane e romane. Con un excursus sui frammenti dogmatici ariani del Mai*, Rome 1902 (Studi e Testi, VII), pp 1-32.

Alcuin/GROW Joint Liturgical Studies

All cost £3.95 (US $8) in 2000—nos. 4 and 16 are out of print

1. (LS 49) Daily and Weekly Worship—from Jewish to Christian by Roger Beckwith
2. (LS 50) The Canons of Hippolytus edited by Paul Bradshaw
3. (LS 51) Modern Anglican Ordination Rites edited by Colin Buchanan
4. (LS 52) Models of Liturgical Theology by James Empereur
5. (LS 53) A Kingdom of Priests: Liturgical Formation of the Laity: The Brixen Essays edited by Thomas Talley
6. (LS 54) The Bishop in Liturgy: an Anglican Study edited by Colin Buchanan
7. (LS 55) Inculturation: the Eucharist in Africa by Phillip Tovey
8. (LS 56) Essays in Early Eastern Initiation edited by Paul Bradshaw,
9. (LS 57) The Liturgy of the Church in Jerusalem by John Baldovin
10. (LS 58) Adult Initiation edited by Donald Withey
11. (LS 59) 'The Missing Oblation': The Contents of the Early Antiochene Anaphora by John Fenwick
12. (LS 60) Calvin and Bullinger on the Lord's Supper by Paul Rorem
13-14 (LS 61) The Liturgical Portions of the Apostolic Constitutions: A Text for Students edited by W. Jardine Grisbrooke (This double-size volume costs double price (i.e. £7.90))
15 (LS 62) Liturgical Inculturation in the Anglican Communion edited by David Holeton
16. (LS 63) Cremation Today and Tomorrow by Douglas Davies
17. (LS 64) The Preaching Service—The Glory of the Methodists by Adrian Burdon
18. (LS 65) Irenaeus of Lyon on Baptism and Eucharist edited with Introduction, Translation and Commentary by David Power
19. (LS 66) Testamentum Domini edited by Grant Sperry-White
20. (LS 67) The Origins of the Roman Rite edited by Gordon Jeanes
21. The Anglican Eucharist in New Zealand 1814-1989 by Bosco Peters
22-23 Foundations of Christian Music: The Music of Pre-Constantinian Christianity by Edward Foley (second double-sized volume at £7.90)
24. Liturgical Presidency by Paul James
25. The Sacramentary of Sarapion of Thmuis: A Text for Students edited by Ric Lennard-Barrett
26. Communion Outside the Eucharist by Phillip Tovey
27. Revising the Eucharist: Groundwork for the Anglican Communion edited by David Holeton
28. Anglican Liturgical Inculturation in Africa edited by David Gitari
29-30. On Baptismal Fonts: Ancient and Modern by Anita Stauffer Geneva (Double-sized volume at £7.90)
31. The Comparative Liturgy of Anton Baumstark by Fritz West
32. Worship and Evangelism in Pre-Christendom by Alan Kreider
33. Liturgy in Early Christian Egypt by Maxwell E. Johnson
34. Welcoming the Baptized by Timothy Turner
35. Daily Prayer in the Reformed Tradition: An Initial Survey by Diane Karay Tripp
36. The Ritual Kiss in Early Christian Worship by Edward Phillips
37. 'After the Primitive Christians': The Eighteenth-century Anglican Eucharist in its Architectural Setting by Peter Doll
38. Coronations Past, Present and Future edited by Paul Bradshaw
39. Anglican Orders and Ordinations edited by David Holeton
40. The Liturgy of St James as presently used edited by Phillip Tovey
41. Anglican Missals by Mark Dalby
42. The Origins of the Roman Rite vol 2 edited by Gordon Jeanes
43. Baptism in Early Byzantine Palestine 325-451 by Juliette Day
44. Ambrosianum Mysterium: the Church of Milan and its Liturgical Tradition Vol. 1 by Cesare Alzati (translated by George Guiver)
45. Mar Nestorius and Mar Theodore the Interpreter: the Forgotten Eucharistic Prayers of East Syria edited by Bryan Spinks